PSALMS AND PRAYERS
FOR
CONGREGATIONAL
PARTICIPATION

B. David Hostetter

Prayers that Paraphrase
Lessons for Each Sunday
in the Christian Year — Series A

Patterned on the Worshipbook
for Presbyterians, Protestants
and Other Christians

1633/ISBN 0-89536-639-8

Dedicated to the memory of my father,

The Reverend Benjamin Hess Hostetter

Who taught me to pray

and used no prayer book

except the Holy Bible

CONTENTS

Acknowledgments vii

Preface ix

Order of Service 1

Advent
First Sunday in Advent 3
Second Sunday in Advent 5
Third Sunday in Advent 7
Fourth Sunday in Advent 9

Christmas
Christmas Eve or Day 11
Christmas Day (Additional Lections) 13
Christmas Day (Additional Lections) 15
First Sunday after Christmas 17
Second Sunday after Christmas 19

Epiphany
The Epiphany 21
Communion Thanksgiving for Epiphany 23
First Sunday after Epiphany 24
Second Sunday after Epiphany 26
Third Sunday after Epiphany 28
Fourth Sunday after Epiphany 30
Fifth Sunday after Epiphany 32
Sixth Sunday after Epiphany 34
Seventh Sunday after Epiphany 36
Eighth Sunday after Epiphany 38
Last Sunday after Epiphany 40

Lent
Ash Wednesday 42
First Sunday in Lent 44
Second Sunday in Lent 46
Third Sunday in Lent 48
Fourth Sunday in Lent 50
Fifth Sunday in Lent 52
Sixth Sunday in Lent (Passion Sunday) 54
Sixth Sunday in Lent (Palm Sunday) 56
Maundy Thursday 58

Easter

Easter Sunday 59
Second Sunday of Easter . . . . : . . 61
Third Sunday of Easter 63
Fourth Sunday of Easter 65
Fifth Sunday of Easter 67
Sixth Sunday of Easter 69
Ascension Day 71
Seventh Sunday of Easter 73

Pentecost

The Day of Pentecost 75
First Sunday after Pentecost (Trinity Sunday) 77
Second Sunday after Pentecost 79
Third Sunday after Pentecost 81
Fourth Sunday after Pentecost 83
Fifth Sunday after Pentecost 85
Sixth Sunday after Pentecost 87
Seventh Sunday after Pentecost 89
Eighth Sunday after Pentecost 91
Ninth Sunday after Pentecost 93
Tenth Sunday after Pentecost 95
Eleventh Sunday after Pentecost 97
Twelfth Sunday after Pentecost 99
Thirteenth Sunday after Pentecost 101
Fourteenth Sunday after Pentecost 103
Fifteenth Sunday after Pentecost 105
Sixteenth Sunday after Pentecost 107
Seventeenth Sunday after Pentecost 109
Eighteenth Sunday after Pentecost 111
Nineteenth Sunday after Pentecost 113
Twentieth Sunday after Pentecost 115
Twenty-first Sunday after Pentecost 117
Twenty-second Sunday after Pentecost 119
Twenty-third Sunday after Pentecost 121
Twenty-fourth Sunday after Pentecost 123
Twenty-fifth Sunday after Pentecost 125
Twenty-sixth Sunday after Pentecost 127
Twenty-seventh Sunday after Pentecost 129
All Saints' Day 131
Thanksgiving Day 133

Index of the Scripture Passages 135

PREFACE

The congregations of Hector and Lodi have prayed many of these prayers with me and read most of these Psalms when we last followed the lectionary Series A. It was not until February 1983 that I discovered that the Consensus Version of the lectionary, prepared by the North American Committee on Calendar and Lectionary, was being recommended by the Consultation on Common Texts for trial use through the next three-year cycle in the churches that have adopted variations of the ecumenical lectionary. The Presbyterian Planning Calendar will display it beginning with Advent 1983. I have re-worked this material, based on an advance copy from the Episcopal Church offices in New York City, and am much obliged to them for a photocopy of what was not yet in print.

I have already signed a contract with C.S.S. Publishing Company for similar materials for Series B, and presumably will revise the Series C volume of *Psalms and Prayers for Congregational Participation* already in print. The revision will be synchronized with the Consensus lectionary, at least for days most often observed in the Reformed tradition.

I have had some helpful feedback from a number of pastors and people who are using the Series C materials, but few have begun to use it with the thoroughness of the Hector-Lodi tradition. To encourage reproduction of these prayers and psalms for congregational participation, we are including a facsimile of a bulletin for a Sunday when Holy Communion was not being celebrated, nor the Sacrament of Baptism administered. I believe prayers and psalms have maximum impact when congregations see, read aloud, and hear others read them at the same time.

The editor of *The Flame,* newsletter for the Coalition on Women and Religion, has characterized my volume for Series C as "semi-sexist." I continue to struggle with a desire to be inclusive in language about people and about God, without being extremist. It is difficult without an inclusive singular personal pronoun that could mean he or she, his or hers, him or her. I have tried "Godself," which does not require advance familiarity, but have not experimented otherwise with innovative pronouns.

Martha Herforth has provided helpful punctuation and occasional re-phrasing to make the prayers more readable by those who did not write them in the first place, or who have not been hearing me or praying with me for years. Mary Lou Warren continues to turn my terrible typing into readable copy. Madge Hostetter has organized the index of Scripture passages for those who wish to use the prayers but do not follow the lectionary on a regular basis.

The Psalms are reproduced from the *Book of Common Prayer,* with no attempt to re-translate them into inclusive language. Where I have paraphrased the Psalms in prayers and other sentences of the liturgy, I have tried to be inclusive.

I welcome comments and suggestions for making future volumes more usable. These may be addressed to me at: P. O. Box 39, Hector, NY 14841 or discussed by telephone: (607) 546-5853. I have introduced with this volume two Eucharistic Prayers patterned after the *Worshipbook* order. Similar ones may follow in future volumes.

ORDER OF SERVICE

GREETING

> Good morning, Good morning
> The Lord be with you,
> AND ALSO WITH YOU.

ANNOUNCEMENTS AND CONCERNS OF THE PEOPLE

CALL TO WORSHIP

*HYMN OF ADORATION: No. 587

PRAYER OF CONFESSION

> Forbearing God, despite your call for absolute obedience and the rejection of all other gods, we continue to follow old customs, unexamined behaviors, not unlike our neighbors, but not in accordance with the teaching of Jesus and contrary to the law of love. Forgive such disloyal behavior that taxes your patience. Give us opportunity to mend our ways as we become aware of our need to repent and follow Jesus more nearly. We ask this in his name. Amen.

ASSURANCE OF PARDON

> Friends, believe the Good News.
> IN JESUS CHRIST, WE ARE FORGIVEN.

ADMONITION

*PASSING OF THE PEACE

FIRST LESSON: 2 Kings 17:33-40

PSALM 33:12-22

> Happy is the nation whose God is the Lord!
> *Happy the people he has chosen to be his own!*
> The Lord looks down from heaven, and holds all the people in the world.
> *From where he sits enthroned he turns his gaze on all who dwell on the earth.*
> He fashions all the hearts of them
> *And understands all their works.*
> There is no king that can be saved by a mighty army.
> *A strong man is not delivered by his great strength.*
> The horse is a vain hope for deliverance;
> *For all its strength it cannot save.*
> Behold, the eye of the Lord is upon those who fear him.
> *On those who wait upon his love,*
> To pluck their lives from death,
> *And to feed them in time of famine.*
> Our soul waits for the Lord;
> *He is our help and our shield.*
> Indeed, our heart rejoices in him,
> *For in his holy name we put our trust.*
> Let your loving-kindness, O Lord, be upon us,
> *As we have put our trust in you.*

*GLORIA

SECOND LESSON: Hebrews 11:1-3, 8-12

GOSPEL: Luke 12:35-40

PRAYER OF THE DAY

> Keep us alert, Good Spirit, dressed for action and looking for the coming of the Son of Man. We will serve you actively in the days of your absence and with greater joy when we are aware of your presence with us. Amen.

SERMON FOR YOUTH: "Unseen Power"

*HYMN: No. 492

SERMON: "Tracking the Unseen"

2

*CREED
*CREED
What is faith? Christian faith is not an opinion or human conviction, but a most firm trust and a clear and steadfast assent of the mind, and then a most certain apprehension of the truth of God presented in the Scriptures and in the Apostles' Creed, and thus also of God himself, the greatest good, and especially of God's promise and of Christ who is the fulfillment of all promises. The Second Helvetic Confession 5.112

PRAYERS OF INTERCESSION

OFFERTORY AND *THE DOXOLOGY

PRAYER OF DEDICATION
Life of our life, God of all goodness, transform these tangibles into the intangibles of the spirit that make the church strong to do your work and accomplish your will in the Spirit of Jesus Christ. Amen.

MINISTRY OF MUSIC

PRAYER OF THANKSGIVING
Jesus, Master, we rejoice in the appreciation you show for the simplest services we render. You have set us a perfect example of selfless service. We honor as well those like Abraham who have followed your leading without knowing your destiny for them. We would give thanks by our daily work as well as by our Sunday liturgy. Praise to you God of Abraham and Sarah. Praise to you, Son of Mary, Son of God. Praise to you, Spirit Eternal, without beginning, without end. Amen.

OUR FATHER IN HEAVEN, HALLOWED BE YOUR NAME,
YOUR KINGDOM COME, YOUR WILL BE DONE, ON EARTH AS IN HEAVEN.
GIVE US TODAY OUR DAILY BREAD.
FORGIVE US OUR SINS AS WE FORGIVE THOSE WHO SIN AGAINST US.
SAVE US FROM THE TIME OF TRIAL, AND DELIVER US FROM EVIL.
FOR THE KINGDOM, THE POWER, AND THE GLORY ARE YOURS NOW
    AND FOREVER. AMEN.

*HYMN: No. 409

THE BENEDICTION

A CHARGE

POSTLUDE

* DENOTES CONGREGATION STAND.

FIRST SUNDAY IN ADVENT

Isaiah 2:1-5   Psalm 122
Romans 13:11-14   Matthew 24:36-44

CALL TO WORSHIP
I rejoice to see you in the house of the Lord, where we come together in unity. Let us give thanks to the Lord himself, and pray for the peace of all earth's cities.

PRAYER OF CONFESSION
Timeless One, you always know what time it is. We become so dulled by the routine that we are often indifferent to the signs of moral decay. Too often we break the monotony by excesses of eating and drinking and sexual adventuring. We play games of one-upmanship, exulting in our superiority, or growing green with jealousy. Forgive our indifference to what such behavior does to others and to ourselves, and our unreadiness for your coming; through Jesus Christ our Lord. Amen.

DECLARATION OF GOD'S FORGIVENESS
Hear the Good News! You have come to the right place, to the house of the Lord, where we pray for each other's good. Friends, believe the Good News. *In Jesus Christ, we are forgiven.*

EXHORTATION
Hold yourselves ready, because the Son of Man will come at the time you least expect him.

PRAYER OF THE DAY
Lord of all history, you alone know all beginnings and all endings. Help us to find our place in your plan of things and to synchronize our time with yours, that we will be ready to do your thing and prepared for your revisitation in Jesus Christ. Amen.

PRAYER OF THANKSGIVING
Supreme Peacemaker, we rejoice in every conversion of the military to the service of the suffering; every use of an army truck to transport relief supplies, every flight of an air force helicopter to rescue the trapped, every naval mission to save those in peril on the sea. We are thankful for the promise of the day when nation shall not point weapons against nation, nor ever again be trained for war. We rejoice in every cooperative effort of nations, and hope for the day of universal peace. You are our Peace, our

Peacemaker, our Inspiration for peacemaking. We praise your name. Amen.

PRAYER OF DEDICATION

Dutiful God, you never fail us. We give thanks to you as is our bounden duty. Receive us, our prayers and our offerings, through your ever-faithful Son, Jesus Christ. Amen.

PSALM 122

I rejoiced when they said to me, "Let us go to the house of the Lord."

Now we stand within your gates, O Jerusalem,

Jerusalem that is built to be a city where people come together in unity;

To which the tribes resort, the tribes of the Lord,

To give thanks to the Lord himself,

The bounden duty of Israel.

For in her are set the thrones of justice,

The thrones of the House of David.

Pray for the peace of Jerusalem: "May those who love you prosper;

Peace be within your ramparts and prosperity in your palaces."

For the sake of these my brothers and my friends, I will say, "Peace be within you."

For the sake of the house of the Lord our God I will pray for your good.

SECOND SUNDAY IN ADVENT

Isaiah 11:1-10   Psalm 72:1-8
Romans 15:4-13   Matthew 3:1-12

CALL TO WORSHIP
With one mind and one voice, praise God, the Parent of our Lord
Jesus Christ, and ours. Glorify God, who is merciful, and sing
hymns to God, who has many names.

PRAYER OF CONFESSION
*Heavenly Sovereign, Scion of the Heavenly House, Spirit of
Wisdom and Power, of what would we repent to prepare the way
for your coming? We confess that there are many things to keep us
busy in preparation for the celebration of Christmas. Have we
allowed too much time for our own parties and too little for
ministries to the sick and the poor? Are we content to be merely
sentimental about the victims of injustice, or do we need to be
more strenuous in our advocacy for them? Have we done enough
to find a common voice in which to both worship you and speak
out against the evils of the world? Turn us back from every evil
way, through Jesus Christ. Amen.*

DECLARATION OF GOD'S FORGIVENESS
Hear the Good News! Jesus Christ baptizes us with the Holy
Spirit and with fire. Friends, believe the Good News! *In Jesus
Christ, we are forgiven.*

EXHORTATION
Agree with one another after the manner of Jesus Christ, so that
with one mind and one voice you may praise the God of the
Gospel.

PRAYER OF THE DAY
*God of wisdom, power and purity, so baptize us with the Holy
Spirit that we may be purged of all that is unfruitful and be taught
by your wisdom, enabled to serve by your strength and be worthy
of worshiping you, through Jesus Christ our Lord. Amen.*

PRAYER OF THANKSGIVING
*God of nature, God in history, God in the church, we give thanks
to you for all that you have created for us to share in our world.
We celebrate every victory of your justice over oppression and
every vindication of the blood of the innocent. We join our voices*

with all who praise your name, in whatever language and whatever style, in every place on earth and in heaven. No human creativity can match the marvelous things that you do. May your glory fill all the earth. Amen.

PRAYER OF DEDICATION

Sovereign of heaven and earth, no gifts of gold and silver, no jewels of earthly value can be as precious to you as the offering of ourselves to you in life and in death. Receive us as worthy, through the acceptance granted to us by Jesus Christ. Amen.

PSALM 72:1-8

Give the King your justice, O God,
And your righteousness to the King's Son;
That he may rule your people righteously
And the poor with justice;
That the mountains may bring prosperity to the people,
And the little hills bring righteousness.
He shall defend the needy among the people;
He shall rescue the poor and crush the oppressor.
He shall live as long as the sun and moon endure,
From one generation to another.
He shall come down like rain upon the mown field,
Like showers that water the earth.
In his time shall the righteous flourish;
There shall be abundance of peace till the moon shall be no more.
He shall rule from sea to sea,
And from the river to the ends of the earth.

THIRD SUNDAY IN ADVENT

Isaiah 35:1-6, 10
James 5:7-10

Psalm 146:5-10
Matthew 11:2-11

CALL TO WORSHIP
You too must be patient and stouthearted, for the coming of the Lord is near.

PRAYER OF CONFESSION
Who are we, Lord God, that we should consider your Son, Jesus, a stumbling-block? And yet we confess that we are impatient for the days of waiting to be over and the day of the final harvest to come. It is not enough for us that surgeons give the blind their sight, hearing aids help the deaf to hear, surgery permits the lame to walk, medicine clears the diseased skin, the stopped heart is started again, the breathless breathe again, and the poor hear the Good News. Forgive us if we want the world made perfect in an instant, with no effort on our part. Pardon our putting the blame on others and not helping others as we can, for the sake of your helping, healing Son, Jesus of Nazareth. Amen.

DECLARATION OF GOD'S FORGIVENESS
Hear the Good News! Happy is the person whose helper is the God of old Israel and new Israel. Our God is king for all generations. The Prince of Life is raised from the dead to give heart to the bereaved and all who face death. Friends, believe the Good News. *In Jesus Christ, we are forgiven.*

EXHORTATION
Strengthen the feeble arms, steady the tottering knees, say to the anxious, be strong and do not be afraid. Your God comes to save you.

PRAYER OF THE DAY
Save us, Honest God, from the smooth-talking religious who would make faith easy and without discipline. Give us insight into the truth, wherever we find it. In however rough form, and whatever the difficulty of the demands it makes on us, may we be faithful to you, despite threat or suffering like that of John the Baptizer and even more like your crucified Son, Jesus, whose living Spirit is with us now. Amen.

PRAYER OF THANKSGIVING

We rejoice and shout for joy, splendid God, that your glory has been revealed in the Gospel of Jesus Christ. We read that Good News with delight; the eyes of the blind are opened, the ears of the deaf unstopped, the lame leap like a deer, and the dumb shout and sing. The crucified is raised from the dead and the living water of the Gospel brings flowers and fruits of faith to the desert of unbelief and meaninglessness. All praise to you, Creator of the human spirit, Healer of the human body, Renewer of the broken spirit. Amen.

PRAYER OF DEDICATION

We show our reverence, God of beauty, truth, and love, with flowers and art, with music and money, with prayers and promises. Receive what we now give and enable us to offer you even finer expressions of our adoration and obedience; like the worshipful Jesus. Amen.

PSALM 146:5-10

Happy is he whose help is the God of Jacob,
Whose hope is in the Lord his God,
Who made heaven and earth, the seas, and all that is in them;
Who keeps his promise for ever;
Who gives justice to those who are oppressed, and food to those
    who hunger,
The Lord sets the prisoners free;
The Lord opens the eyes of the blind;
The Lord lifts up those who are bowed down;
The Lord loves the righteous; the Lord cares for the stranger;
He sustains the orphan and widow, but frustrates the way of the
    wicked.
The Lord shall reign for ever,
Your God, O Zion, throughout all generations. Hallelujah!

FOURTH SUNDAY IN ADVENT

Isaiah 7:10-16   Psalm 24
Romans 1:1-7   Matthew 1:18-25

CALL TO WORSHIP

Beloved of God and called to holiness, grace and peace from God our Father and the Lord Jesus Christ. Seek the face of God, for God is with us.

PRAYER OF CONFESSION

God ahead of us, God behind us, God with us, forgive our lack of expectation as we come to your house. We overlook many signs of your presence, or take them for granted, and are not inspired to look for further signs of your coming. Having sometimes ignored our calling to holiness, we have not been candid about our sin and need for grace. Surprise us with twinges of conscience that will make our confession more honest and our forgiveness, genuine peace; through Jesus Christ. Amen.

DECLARATION OF GOD'S FORGIVENESS

Hear the Good News. Mary has conceived a child by the Holy Spirit and he is to be named Jesus, for he shall save his people from their sins. Friends, believe the Good News. *In Jesus Christ, we are forgiven.*

EXHORTATION

Ascend the mountain of the Lord, and stand in his holy place with heart and hands that have been cleansed. Descend again to spread the Good News that God's Son, a descendant of David, humanly speaking, receives both Jews and gentiles who believe in him.

PRAYER OF THE DAY

God of Jesus, Mary and Joseph, grant us such humble faith that we may do what you direct, whatever the consequences, knowing that your intentions are always loving, though not always accomplished without misunderstanding and grief; for your kingdom's sake. Amen.

PRAYER OF THANKSGIVING

King of Glory, Prince of Peace, glorious and peaceful Spirit, we rejoice with the wise and the seekers of every nation and race who

10

have sought your face and found you near. We thank you for the true promise of the prophets, for the faithful naming of Jesus of David's line, Immanuel, a Divine Savior, Son of Mary, Son of God. With angels and apostles, with prophets and priests, with young and old, with people of all nations, we rejoice that Immanuel has been glorified by resurrection from the dead. We have received this ineffable blessing from you. Alleluia. Amen.

PRAYER OF DEDICATION
The fullness of the earth and the seas is yours, Creator of all things, personal and impersonal. Receive us with our gifts, for we are also yours. Sanctify us and our gifts in your service, that the name of Jesus may be honored. Amen.

PSALM 24
The earth is the Lord's and all that is in it,
The world and those who dwell therein.
For it was he who founded it upon the seas
And planted it firm upon the waters beneath.
Who may go up the mountain of the Lord?
And who may stand in his holy place?
He who has clean hands and a pure heart,
Who has not set his mind on falsehood, and has not committed perjury.
He shall receive a blessing from the Lord,
And justice from God his savior.
Such is the fortune of those who seek him,
Who seek the face of the God of Jacob.
Lift up your heads, you gates,
Lift yourselves up, you everlasting doors, that the King of Glory may come in.
Who is the king of glory?
The Lord strong and mighty,
The Lord mighty in battle.
Lift up your heads, you gates,
Lift them up, you everlasting doors, that the king of glory may come in.
Who then is the king of glory?
The king of glory is the Lord of Hosts.

CHRISTMAS EVE OR DAY

Isaiah 9:2-7   Psalm 96
Titus 2:11-14   Luke 2:1-20

CALL TO WORSHIP

Bow down to the Lord of heaven and earth, dance and sing in his honor, all angels and earthlings.

PRAYER OF CONFESSION

Gracious God, Healing God and Savior, Dawning Spirit, set us free from our wickedness, making us a pure people eager to do good. We confess that we do not always live temperately, sometimes stretching the truth, frequently neglecting our prayers, and forgetful of the great day when the splendor of our great God and Savior Jesus Christ shall appear. Forgive our worldliness and sin, for the sake of Jesus, our Savior. Amen.

DECLARATION OF GOD'S FORGIVENESS

Hear the Good News! The grace of God has dawned upon the world with healing for all humanity! Friends, believe the Good News! *In Jesus Christ, we are forgiven.*

EXHORTATION

Speak with authority when you are urging and arguing for truly Christian themes, and let no one slight you when you share your Christian faith.

PRAYER OF THE DAY

Supreme Sovereign, when you take your divine census, count us among the brothers and sisters of Jesus Christ, making wherever we live also the hometown of Jesus Christ, a place where he abides with us in the Spirit, so that your realm is extended everywhere in the world. Amen.

PRAYER OF THANKSGIVING

Human Star of Bethlehem, you shine with the glory of the dawn in the darkness of our sinful world. Thanks be to God. Creator of heaven and earth, you send us a Prince of Peace, a boy born for us, a son given to us bearing the symbol of your authority over humanity. Thanks be to God. Timeless One, you establish and sustain justice and righteousness in all the earth. Thanks be to God. For all born and baptized in your name in the year that is past, we declare our thanksgiving. With all creation we exult in

your might and beauty, your majesty and splendor. You are great
and worthy of all praise. Amen.

PRAYER OF DEDICATION

Jesus Christ, God and Savior, no gift of ours can match the
sacrifice of yourself for us. We are yours by baptism, marked as
your own, so receive our gifts as a sign of our willing service and
our eagerness to do good in your name. Amen.

PSALM 96

Sing to the Lord a new song;
Sing to the Lord, all the whole earth.
Sing to the Lord and bless his Name;
Proclaim the good news of his salvation from day to day.
Declare his glory among the nations
And his wonders among all peoples.
For great is the Lord and greatly to be praised;
He is more to be feared than all gods.
As for all the gods of the nations, they are but idols;
But it is the Lord who made the heavens.
Oh, the majesty and magnificence of his presence!
Oh, the power and the splendor of his sanctuary!
Ascribe to the Lord, you families of the peoples;
Ascribe to the Lord honor and power.
Ascribe to the Lord the honor due his Name;
Bring offerings and come into his courts.
Worship the Lord in the beauty of holiness;
Let the whole earth tremble before him.
Tell it out among the nations: "The Lord is King!
*He has made the world so firm that it cannot be moved; he will
    judge the peoples with equity."*
Let the heavens rejoice, and let the earth be glad;
*Let the sea thunder and all that is in it; let the field be joyful and
    all that is therein.*
Then shall all the trees of the wood shout for joy before the Lord
    when he comes,
When he comes to judge the earth.
He will judge the world with righteousness
And the peoples with his truth.

CHRISTMAS DAY
Additional Lections

Isaiah 62:6-7, 10-12   Psalm 97
Titus 3:4-7   Luke 2:8-20

CALL TO WORSHIP
I have Good News for you: there is great joy coming to the
whole people. Today in the city of David a deliverer has been
born to you — the Messiah, the Lord.

PRAYER OF CONFESSION
*God of the Gospel, whose glory brightens the night sky on Christ-
mas Eve, and the birth of whose Son by Mary in Bethlehem brings
the dawn of a new day, hear our prayers for forgiveness and mercy.
Pardon us if we have made idols of what are only symbols of the
coming of Jesus, if a traditional practice has defined the meaning
of today, rather than the reality of the coming of Jesus Christ. We
can appeal to your kindness and generosity, not for any good
deeds of our own, but because of our salvation through the water
of baptism and the renewing power of the Holy Spirit. By your
grace, Jesus Christ is our Savior. Amen.*

DECLARATION OF GOD'S FORGIVENESS
Hear the Good News! God in highest heaven grants peace on
earth to all on whom rests the favor of the Most High. Friends,
believe the Good News! *In Jesus Christ, we are forgiven.*

EXHORTATION
Raise a signal to all peoples. This is God's proclamation to
earth's farthest bounds.

PRAYER OF THE DAY
*Exalted One, having received the Good News of Jesus Christ with
great joy, we would be sent like the shepherds to astonish others
with the story of Jesus and the meaning of our salvation through
his grace. Amen.*

PRAYER OF THANKSGIVING
*God in highest heaven, we give you thanks for the sending of Jesus
Christ into our world to be a gift of peace, a person of peace, a
Prince of Peace. Christ most lowly, we give thanks for your
humble birth and gracious life, for salvation and the hope of
eternal life. Spirit most holy, we thank you for the water of rebirth*

14

and the renewal of the spirit thus signified, by which we are saved, being justified by the grace of our Lord Jesus Christ. All glory be ascribed to you, One God, giving, coming, renewing. Amen.

PRAYER OF DEDICATION

Holy Child of God and of Mary Virgin, heaven and earth are your homes, temple and stable are hallowed by your presence. We bring our gifts to you so that the Good News of peace may continue to sound in earth and heaven, echoed by human voices, the voice of your church. Amen.

PSALM 97

The Lord is King; let the earth rejoice;
Let the multitude of the isles be glad.
Clouds and darkness are round about him,
Righteousness and justice are the foundations of his throne.
A fire goes before him and burns up his enemies on every side.
His lightnings light up the world; the earth sees it and is afraid.
The mountains melt like wax at the presence of the Lord,
At the presence of the Lord of the whole earth.
The heavens declare his righteousness,
And all the peoples see his glory.
Confounded be all who worship carved images and delight in false Gods!
Bow down before him, all you gods,
Zion hears and is glad, and the cities of Judah rejoice, because of your judgments, O Lord.
For you are the Lord, most high over all the earth; you are exalted far above all gods.
The Lord loves those who hate evil;
He preserves the lives of his saints and delivers them from the hand of the wicked.
Light has sprung up for the righteous,
And joyful gladness for those who are truehearted.
Rejoice in the Lord, you righteous,
And give thanks to his holy Name.

CHRISTMAS DAY
Additional Lections

Isaiah 52:7-10   Psalm 98
Hebrews 1:1-12   John 1:1-14

CALL TO WORSHIP
Sing a new song to our Sovereign God, who has done marvelous
deeds. Break into songs of joy in God's honor with all kinds of
musical instruments.

PRAYER OF CONFESSION
*God of power beyond our imagining, who has created a universe
beyond our measuring, but not beyond our spoiling, forgive us if
we occupy or use any part of the world for other than your glory.
Personal God, beyond all definition, excuse us if we attempt to
confine you within the descriptions of our best language, and miss
your essential being as expressed in Jesus Christ. Universal God,
whose life lights all persons everywhere, pardon the limitations we
may seek to make on your influence in the lives of people
throughout the world. Hear our prayer in the name of Jesus Christ.
Amen.*

DECLARATION OF GOD'S FORGIVENESS
Hear the Good News! To all who receive Jesus Christ, full of
grace and truth, God gives the right to become children of God,
the offspring of Godself. Friends, believe the Good News. *In
Jesus Christ, we are forgiven.*

EXHORTATION
Let your feet take you to any place where you can herald the
Good News of God's truth and grace in Jesus Christ.

PRAYER OF THE DAY
*Modest God, help us to recognize the grace and truth, fully
manifest in Jesus Christ, and also the real light that enlightens all
who are in the world, that the darkness may be rolled back and
more light shine out everywhere in the world. Amen.*

PRAYER OF THANKSGIVING
*Creating Word, we celebrate beginnings, the beginnings of time
and space, the creation of all beings, of all things animate and
inanimate. Saving Word, we give thanks for the Word become
flesh to dwell among us full of grace and truth, the offspring of*

16

God, but with the human name of salvation, Jesus, Savior. Sustaining Word, we praise the incredible power that maintains the universe, that makes a faith-family of all who receive Jesus, God's special Child. Glory be to you, O God, with whom was the Word in the beginning, and who is your Last Word. Amen.

PRAYER OF DEDICATION

No gift of yours can match your priceless gift to the whole world at the first Christmas, Giving God, but use our offerings and ourselves to gather a growing family of people receiving Jesus as your gracious Son and our Brother. Amen.

PSALM 98

Sing to the Lord a new song, for he has done marvelous things.
With his right hand and his holy arm has he won for himself the
    victory.
The Lord has made known his victory;
His righteousness has he openly shown in the sight of the nations.
He remembers his mercy and faithfulness to the house of Israel,
And all the ends of the earth have seen the victory of our God.
Shout with joy to the Lord, all you lands;
Lift up your voice, rejoice, and sing.
Sing to the Lord with the harp,
With the harp and the voice of song.
With trumpets and the sound of the horn shout with joy before
    the King, the Lord.
Let the sea make a noise and all that is in it, the lands and those
    who dwell therein.
Let the rivers clap their hands, and let the hills ring out with joy
    before the Lord, when he comes to judge the earth.
In righteousness shall he judge the world and the peoples with
    equity.

FIRST SUNDAY AFTER CHRISTMAS

Isaiah 63:7-9   Psalm 111
Hebrews 2:10-18   Matthew 2:13-15, 19-23

CALL TO WORSHIP
With the whole congregation we will praise the great doings of
God, who has won a name by marvelous deeds.

PRAYER OF CONFESSION
*God for all nations, we live still in a world where fathers and
mothers and children must seek refuge from violence and
bloodshed. We have learned little of the ways of peace,
depending on the power of armaments to maintain governments
and not sparing even children in the massacres of war. Forgive us
if we have been advocates of war or indifferent to the needs of
refugees. We need to learn more just ways of settling claims to
govern and more equitable distribution of the good things you
have created for us all to enjoy. Free us all to serve each other in
Christ-like tenderness, for your Name's sake. Amen.*

DECLARATION OF GOD'S FORGIVENESS
Hear the Good News! Jesus Christ has become like us in every
way, so that he might be merciful and faithful as our high priest
before God, expiating our sins. Friends, believe the Good News.
In Jesus Christ, we are forgiven.

EXHORTATION
Meet whatever tests face you now, knowing that Jesus is able to
help us, having passed through the test of suffering.

PRAYER OF THE DAY
*Whether in withdrawal or return, Great Overseer, help us to fulfill
your purposes for us as individuals and as families,
acknowledging our need for each other and always seeking what
is best for all of us. Give us patience to retreat and wait for the
right time and courage to advance and confront when that is in
line with your plans for us and for others; through your carpenter-
Son, Jesus of Nazareth. Amen.*

PRAYER OF THANKSGIVING
*God above time, God in our history, God in our present, we are
thankful that you govern the times and seasons. Our times are in
your hands, and we are grateful for times of joy as well as sorrow,*

for dancing as well as mourning, for the time of Christ's birth as well as his death. Our own families know these cycles of changes as generations rise and pass away. We rejoice in the babies, the children and grandchildren among us and in the long life which allows many of us to see them grow up. Hear our praise, in voices young and old, high and low, weak and strong, until our time of silence comes. Amen.

PRAYER OF DEDICATION

High God, you have not merely sent an angelic envoy to us, but have come yourself to deliver us through Jesus Christ. We stand before you to offer ourselves and not merely our offerings to serve you and others as one people, your people. Amen.

PSALM 111

Hallelujah! I will give thanks to the Lord with my whole heart,
In the assembly of the upright in the congregation.
Great are the deeds of the Lord!
They are studied by all who delight in them,
His work is full of majesty and splendor,
And his righteousness endures for ever.
He makes his marvelous works to be remembered;
The Lord is gracious and full of compassion.
He gives food to those who fear him;
He is ever mindful of his covenant.
He has shown his people the power of his works in giving them
the lands of the nations.
The works of his hands are faithfulness and justice;
All his commandments are sure.
*They stand fast for ever and ever, because they are done in truth
and equity.*
He sent redemption to his people;
*He commanded his covenant for ever; holy and awesome is his
Name.*
The fear of the Lord is the beginning of wisdom;
*Those who act accordingly have a good understanding; his praise
endures for ever.*

SECOND SUNDAY AFTER CHRISTMAS

Jeremiah 31:7-14   Psalm 147:12-20
Ephesians 1:3-6, 15-18   John 1:1-18

CALL TO WORSHIP
You have the right to become children of God through receiving
Jesus Christ as God's only Son, full of grace and truth.

PRAYER OF CONFESSION
*All-glorious God, paternal, fraternal, maternal, though we have
faith in Jesus Christ and love toward your people, yet we are not
without blemish in your sight, not full of love, wisdom, and other
spiritual blessings you still have available for us. Our love is not as
inclusive as yours, and there is much we need to learn. Give us a
clearer vision of all that we are meant to be, so that by becoming
fulfilled, we may increase the glory that is properly revealed in
Jesus Christ, your Beloved. Amen.*

DECLARATION OF GOD'S FORGIVENESS
Hear the Good News! Of those who have seen God, God's only
Son, Jesus, nearest the Father's heart, makes God known most
clearly. Out of the full store of heavenly favor, we have received
grace upon grace. Friends, believe the Good News! *In Jesus
Christ, we are forgiven.*

EXHORTATION
Open your eyes to all to which God calls you, the wealth and
glory you are offered among God's people.

PRAYER OF THE DAY
*God of Moses and of Jesus, give us clear understanding of your
purposes, in law and Gospel, so that without confusion we may
bear witness: "grace and truth came through Jesus Christ." Amen.*

PRAYER OF THANKSGIVING
*God of all seasons, God of many nations, we rejoice in the
beauties of winter and spring, summer and fall. We celebrate your
great revelations to Israel through Moses and the prophets, and
the spread of the Good News of Jesus Christ through apostles and
the church. Young and old rejoice together in varieties of music
and even in the liveliness of dance. You turn mourning into
gladness and fill our hearts with overflowing joy. Thanks be to
you, O God, for law and grace, for promise and fulfillment, for*

20

hope and hope and hope. Amen.

PRAYER OF DEDICATION
Gracious Householder, as you have received us graciously at our homecoming, we offer our work and witness to make the way smooth for others who may also find their way here to receive your comfort and love. Amen.

PSALM 147:12-20
The Lord has pleasure in those who fear him,
In those who await his gracious favor.
Worship the Lord, O Jerusalem;
Praise your God, O Zion;
For he has strengthened the bars of your gates;
He has blessed your children within you.
He has established peace on your borders;
He satisfies you with the finest wheat.
He sends out his command to the earth,
And his word runs very swiftly.
He gives snow like wool;
He scatters hoarfrost like ashes.
He scatters his hail like bread crumbs;
Who can stand against his cold?
He sends forth his word and melts them;
He blows with his wind, and the waters flow.
He declares his word to Jacob,
His statutes and his judgments to Israel.

EPIPHANY

Isaiah 60:1-6   Psalm 72:1-14
Ephesians 3:1-6   Matthew 2:1-12

CALL TO WORSHIP
Arise, people of God, rise clothed in light. God's light has come
and the glory of Jesus Christ shines over you.

PRAYER OF CONFESSION
*Eternal Sovereign, you rule us with such freedom as to permit our
choice of light or darkness, justice or oppression, peace or
violence, pity or neglect of the poor and the suffering. Forgive our
alliance with those who make wrong choices, as well as the wrong
choices we have made on our own. Deliver us from oppression or
being oppressors. Pardon our sins and free us to serve you fully,
now and always. Amen.*

DECLARATION OF GOD'S FORGIVENESS
Hear the Good News! The secret has been revealed. The Gospel
makes Gentiles joint heirs with Jews of the promise made in
Christ Jesus. Friends, believe the Good News! *In Jesus Christ, we
are forgiven.*

EXHORTATION
Share news of the gift of God's grace in Christ for the benefit of
others.

PRAYER OF THE DAY
*God of stars, moons, and all planets, so guide us to where you are
that we may give gifts to the Christ when giving food to the
hungry, drink to the thirsty, clothing to the naked, and making
visits to the sick and the imprisoned. Having visited you in visiting
them, we ask to be received at last into eternal life, through Jesus
Christ our Lord. Amen.*

PRAYER OF THANKSGIVING
*God of Israel and all nations, we give thanks to you for the wise
and the wisdom of all nations. Child of Bethlehem and heaven, we
give thanks for all children in the care of loving parents, and all
who care for children when parents cannot. Universal Spirit, we
give thanks for gifts of music and art and dance that can be
enjoyed by people of all languages without need for translation.
For all that draws us together as one human family, we give thanks*

to you, our Parent, our Brother Jesus, our Family Spirit, one God.
Amen.

PRAYER OF DEDICATION

*Before cradle or throne, Lord Jesus, we present our gifts, not as
exotic as gold and frankincense and myrrh, but expressions of our
homage nonetheless, and ask that you will receive them and us as
dedicated to your royal service. Amen.*

PSALM 72:1-14

Give the King your justice, O God,
And your righteousness to the King's Son;
That he may rule your people righteously
And the poor with justice;
That the mountains may bring prosperity to the people,
And the little hills bring righteousness.
He shall defend the needy among the people;
He shall rescue the poor and crush the oppressor.
He shall live as long as the sun and moon endure,
From one generation to another.
He shall come down like rain upon the mown field,
Like showers that water the earth.
In his time shall the righteous flourish;
There shall be abundance of peace till the moon shall be no more.
He shall rule from sea to sea,
And from the River to the ends of the earth.
His foes shall bow down before him,
And his enemies lick the dust.
The kings of Tarshish and of the isles shall pay tribute,
And the kings of Arabia and Saba offer gifts.
All kings shall bow down before him,
And all the nations do him service.
For he shall deliver the poor who cries out in distress,
And the oppressed who has no helper.
He shall have pity on the lowly and poor;
He shall preserve the lives of the needy.
He shall redeem their lives from oppression and violence,
And dear shall their blood be in his sight.

COMMUNION THANKSGIVING FOR EPIPHANY SEASON

God of Light, in whom there is no darkness at all, nor shadow of turning, we thank you for the manifestation of your invisible glory, through the coming of the Prince of Light, Son of Mary, born under the Bethlehem star, to enter the human arena and become our champion against the prince of darkness. In the worship of Jesus, we join with the simple and the wise, with the poor and the rich, with Jew and Gentile. For the gift of the Spirit by which you acknowledge your beloved Son and all your beloved children in every age, we give you sincere thanks and praise.

Great and marvelous are your deeds, Sovereign over all. Just and true are your ways, Ruler of the ages. Who shall not revere you and do homage to your name? For you alone are holy. All nations shall come and worship in your presence, for your just dealings stand revealed.

Holy, holy, holy is God, the sovereign of all, who was, and is, and is to come!

Light unapproachable, we thank you for the Light of lights, manifest to the whole world, Jew and Gentile, in Jesus of Nazareth, born in Bethlehem, circumcised in Jerusalem, a son of the law, baptized by John in the Jordan, calling disciples, teaching all who would hear, healing the sick, casting out mental darkness, declaring forgiveness of sins. We celebrate the light that shines on in the dark; the darkness has never mastered it.

We celebrate the life that survives death in resurrection, the Easter dawn that sends light streaming into the valley of the shadow of death.

With John the Baptizer we bear witness to the light, the real light which enlightens everyone even now coming into the world.

With the church everywhere, we break the bread and drink the cup that manifest his gift of saving life and eternal light to all believers.

Holy Spirit, descend on us and touch us with new fire and light, so that this table that is spread shall bring new energies to our spirits, new radiance to our lives, new power to our witness.

FIRST SUNDAY AFTER EPIPHANY
Baptism of the Lord

Isaiah 42:1-9   Psalm 29
Acts 10:34-43   Matthew 3:13-17

CALL TO WORSHIP
Ascribe to the Lord the glory due to his name; bow down to the
Lord in the splendor of holiness.

PRAYER OF CONFESSION
*God of life and light and love, we confess that our own lives are
too dear to us. By comparison, we do not want for others as much
as we want for ourselves. We want justice and power for our party
or nation, but not for all parties and nations. We have some
concern for our own enlightenment but not for the enlightenment
of all people everywhere. Sometimes we need to have patience
with ourselves; more often, patience with others. Forgive the
narrowness of our vision and of our commitment to others and to
you, Creator of life, Light of our eyes, universal Spirit of justice.
Amen.*

DECLARATION OF GOD'S FORGIVENESS
Hear the Good News of peace through Jesus Christ, who is Lord
of all. It is to him that all the prophets testify, declaring that
everyone who trusts in him receives forgiveness of sins through
his name. Friends, believe the Good News. *In Jesus Christ, we are
forgiven.*

EXHORTATION
God has commanded the church to proclaim Jesus Christ to the
people and to affirm that he is the one who has been designated
by God as judge of the living and the dead.

PRAYER OF THE DAY
*Condescending God, we also would conform to all that you
require, both being baptized and baptizing in the name of God,
Father, Son, and Holy Spirit. Grant us the assurance that we are
your children, blessed and beloved, that we may obey you with
joy. Amen.*

PRAYER OF THANKSGIVING
*God of everywhere and anywhere, we thank you for Jesus of
Nazareth and for all to whom he relates us, not only the apostles*

and Cornelius the Centurion in past centuries, but also the
Godfearing of every nation in our own time. We celebrate the
Good News of Jesus, that he went about doing good and healing
all who were sick in mind, body or spirit. We remember with
devotion the death on the cross for us and rising from the dead,
witnessed by the apostles and women of faith, chosen in advance.
We ascribe to you creativity, caring, and covenanting, giving us
life, granting us healing and forgiveness, gathering us into the
church of Jesus Christ. Amen.

PRAYER OF DEDICATION
God of glory, we respond to all you have spoken, in the wonders
of nature, in the words of the Scriptures, in the Word made human
to dwell among us. We glorify you in the presentation of flowers
and funds, words and music, and by our presence in this
sanctuary, in the name of Jesus Christ. Amen.

PSALM 29
Ascribe to the Lord, you gods,
Ascribe to the Lord glory and strength.
Ascribe to the Lord the glory due his Name;
Worship the Lord in the beauty of holiness.
The voice of the Lord is upon the waters, the God of glory
thunders;
The Lord is upon the mighty waters.
The voice of the Lord is a powerful voice;
The voice of the Lord is a voice of splendor.
The voice of the Lord breaks the cedar trees;
The Lord breaks the cedars of Lebanon;
He makes Lebanon skip like a calf,
And Mount Hermon like a young wild ox.
The voice of the Lord splits the flames of fire; the voice of the
Lord shakes the wilderness;
The Lord shakes the wilderness of Kadesh.
The voice of the Lord makes the oak trees writhe and strips the
forests bare.
And in the temple of the Lord all are crying, "Glory!"
The Lord sits enthroned above the flood;
The Lord sits enthroned as King for evermore.
The Lord shall give strength to his people;
The Lord shall give his people the blessing of peace.

SECOND SUNDAY AFTER EPIPHANY

Isaiah 49:1-7   Psalm 40:1-11
1 Corinthians 1:1-9   John 1:29-34

CALL TO WORSHIP
Do not keep the goodness of God hidden in your heart: proclaim
God's faithfulness and saving power.

PRAYER OF CONFESSION
*Supremely powerful Person, you have shown us love as well as
awesome strength. In Jesus of Nazareth you have come among us
as one who serves. We confess that we often prefer to be served
than to serve, to be masters rather than servants. Forgive our
disposition to shirk your service when we may risk suffering in the
hands of the cruel and uncaring. To be sent as lambs among
wolves does not appeal to us, as it did not appeal to Jesus, who
nevertheless was your lamb to take away the sins of the world,
including ours. Amen.*

DECLARATION OF GOD'S FORGIVENESS
Hear the Good News. You are claimed as Christ's own along with
everyone who invokes the name of our Lord Jesus Christ. Friends,
believe the Good News. *In Jesus Christ, we are forgiven.*

EXHORTATION
Go in God's strength to call back those who have turned away
from God and the people of God. Be a light to all who live in the
shadows.

PRAYER OF THE DAY
*Baptize us with the Holy Spirit, divine Baptizer, that the Spirit of
peace may abide with us, drawing us together despite the
differences and distances between us. Gather us into unity in your
church, to the glory of your name and the name of Jesus, who also
accepted baptism for our sake. Amen.*

PRAYER OF THANKSGIVING
*You have done many wonderful things for us, masterful God. You
have freed us from traps and situations that frightened us. You
have sent us on our way again with new plans for our future. We
share with others the Good News that you save all who put their
trust in you. We praise you before others and seek to warn those
who might fall into temptations that have threatened our lives.*

Your love and loyalty will always uphold us, faithful Sovereign,
brave Champion, Emissary of peace. Amen.

PRAYER OF DEDICATION

Founder of the church, when we are unsure of accomplishing
anything as your people, you promise to renew our light, that our
witness may be seen by many. Receive our moneys and all our
talents of hand and heart and voice, to spread the Good News of
your grace and peace. Amen.

PSALM 40:1-11

I waited patiently upon the Lord;
He stooped to me and heard my cry.

He lifted me out of the desolate pit, out of the mire and clay;
He set my feet upon a high cliff and made my footing sure.

He put a new song in my mouth,
A song of praise to our God;

Many shall see, and stand in awe,
And put their trust in the Lord.

Happy are they who trust in the Lord!
They do not resort to evil spirits or turn to false gods.

Great things are they that you have done, O Lord my God!
How great your wonders and your plans for us!

There is none who can be compared with you.
Oh, that I could make them known and tell them! But they are
  more than I can count.

In sacrifice and offering you take no pleasure (you have given me
  ears to hear you);
Burnt-offering and sin-offering you have not required, and so I
  said, "Behold, I come.

In the roll of the book it is written concerning me: "I love to do
  your will, O my God; your law is deep in my heart.' "

I proclaimed righteousness in the great congregation; behold, I
  did not restrain my lips; and that, O Lord, you know.

Your righteousness have I not hidden in my heart; I have spoken
  of your faithfulness and your deliverance;
I have not concealed your love and faithfulness from the great
  congregation.

THIRD SUNDAY AFTER EPIPHANY

Isaiah 9:1-4   Psalm 27:1-6
1 Corinthians 1:10-17   Matthew 4:12-23

CALL TO WORSHIP

Be constant in the house of the Lord all the days of your life.
Gaze upon the beauty of the Lord and seek him in his temple.

PRAYER OF CONFESSION

*Lord Jesus Christ, we confess that we have dishonored your name
by our quarrels and divisions. We have frequently bragged about
our own denominations at the expense of other denominations.
We have guessed at the opinions and beliefs of others, without the
patience to ask and to listen to them in order to understand. Too
often we have stressed our differences, without any appreciation
of our common faith and baptism. Forgive such pride that
projects our own "wisdom" and clouds the Gospel of your cross
for your own name's sake. Amen.*

DECLARATION OF GOD'S FORGIVENESS

Hear the Good News! Christ has not been divided among us. He
was crucified for us all. We are not divided by our baptism by
whomever we were baptized. Friends, believe the Good News. *In
Jesus Christ, we are forgiven.*

EXHORTATION

Agree among yourselves and avoid divisions. Be firmly joined in
unity of mind and thought. We are all followers of Jesus of
Nazareth.

PRAYER OF THE DAY

*Divine Educator, teach us in our churches. Proclaimer of the
kingdom, preach to us in our chapels. Sacred Healer, cure us of
our illnesses and infirmities. Light of eternity, dawn on all who
dwell in the land of death's dark shadow. Amen.*

PRAYER OF THANKSGIVING

*Light too dazzling for human eyes, Light in focus in human form,
Light dispersed in human beings, you have increased our joy and
given us great gladness. You have freed those who were oppressed
and given new dignity to those who were demeaned. You have
brought light and freedom where there has been constraint and
gloom. You have gathered children of light wherever the Good*

News is preached, and sent them out as lightbearers to those living still in the land of death's dark shadow. We rejoice with all who have seen the light and known your healing and ingathering. Amen.

PRAYER OF DEDICATION

You may be worshiped in tent or tabernacle, in temple or house, God-Everywhere. We will acclaim you with sacrifices of praise and offerings to maintain this house of prayer; to the glory of your name, Parent above all, ever-loving Brother, familial Spirit. Amen.

PSALM 27:1-6

The Lord is my light and my salvation; whom then shall I fear?
The Lord is the strength of my life; of whom then shall I be afraid?
When evildoers came upon me to eat up my flesh,
It was they, my foes and my adversaries, who stumbled and fell.
Though an army should encamp against me, yet my heart shall not be afraid;
And though war should rise up against me, yet will I put my trust in him.
One thing have I asked of the Lord;
One thing I seek;
That I may dwell in the house of the Lord all the days of my life;
To behold the fair beauty of the Lord and to seek him in his temple.

FOURTH SUNDAY AFTER EPIPHANY

Micah 6:1-8   Psalm 37:1-11
1 Corinthians 1:18-3l   Matthew 5:1-12

CALL TO WORSHIP
Depend upon God to grant your heart's desire. Commit your life
to Christ and trust the Spirit to do what is beyond your doing.

PRAYER OF CONFESSION
*Wise and mighty God, humble and gentle God, humbling and
gentling Spirit, we confess that we do not always learn without
pride, nor act with self-control. We forget the example of Jesus,
who taught without arrogance and acted without domineering.
Forgive us for undue regard for human standards of scholarship
or rank or office, whether in others or ourselves. Excuse our proud
boast of accomplishments that discounts what we owe to you and
others and disregards the gap between our finiteness and your
infinity. How foolish and weak we can be. Amen.*

DECLARATION OF GOD'S FORGIVENESS
Hear the Good News! God has made Christ our wisdom and
righteousness and in him we are consecrated and free. Friends,
believe the Good News. *In Jesus Christ, we are forgiven.*

EXHORTATION
If you boast at all, let your boasting be about the Lord Jesus, who
is God's wisdom and power.

PRAYER OF THE DAY
*All-blessing God, in our search for happiness, save us from the
expediency of the moment, the exploitation of the weak, and the
exercise of selfish rights, that we may know the rewards that last,
the mercy you offer the merciful and the peace of your presence,
through Jesus Christ our Teacher. Amen.*

PRAYER OF THANKSGIVING
*God of the Gospel, Christ of the cross, Voice of the Scriptures, we
rejoice in the wisdom of the eternal that you share with the
humble. We accept with gratitude the salvation you offer to those
who have faith in the doctrine of the cross. We celebrate with joy
the overthrow of all that exalts itself against you. Let our boasting
always be in what you do for us in suffering love and gentle
wisdom and overflowing mercy. Amen.*

PRAYER OF DEDICATION

What shall we bring when we approach you, O God? How shall we bow down before the Most High? No offerings can atone for our sins. Christ has offered himself for us. Enable us to act justly, to love mercy and to walk humbly before you, in the Spirit of Jesus Christ. Amen.

PSALM 37:1-11

Do not fret yourself because of evildoers;
Do not be jealous of those who do wrong.
For they shall soon wither like the grass,
And like the green grass fade away.
Put your trust in the Lord and do good;
Dwell in the land and feed on its riches.
Take delight in the Lord, and he shall give you your heart's desire.
Commit your way to the Lord and put your trust in him, and he will bring it to pass.
He will make your righteousness as clear as the light
And your just dealing as the noonday.
Be still before the Lord
And wait patiently for him.
Do not fret yourself over the one who prospers, the one who succeeds in evil schemes.
Refrain from anger, leave rage alone; do not fret yourself; it leads only to evil.
For evildoers shall be cut off,
But those who wait upon the Lord shall possess the land.
In a little while the wicked shall be no more;
You shall search out their place, but they will not be there.
But the lowly shall possess the land;
They will delight in abundance of peace.

FIFTH SUNDAY AFTER EPIPHANY

Isaiah 58:3-10   Psalm 112:4-9
1 Corinthians 2:1-11   Matthew 5:13-16

CALL TO WORSHIP
O praise the Lord! Happy is the person who fears the Lord and finds great joy in his commandments.

PRAYER OF CONFESSION
Creator — Restorer — Ruler: We are prone to point the finger at others and to pervert justice by exaggerated charges. We want the rich to feed the hungry, but not to share from our own provisions. We prefer charity in principle, but in practice evade our duty even to our own kin. Some of us live in half-empty houses while there are families crowded into rooms too small for them, if they have rooms at all. Forgive our failure to live up to the best we know and to let the oppressed go free even after you have freed us. Amen.

DECLARATION OF GOD'S FORGIVENESS
Hear the Good News! Our faith is not built on human wisdom but on the power of God. Christ nailed to the cross attests the cost of God's love and forgiveness. Friends, believe the Good News! *In Jesus Christ, we are forgiven.*

EXHORTATION
You must shed light among your neighbors so that when they see the good you do, they may give praise to your heavenly Parent.

PRAYER OF THE DAY
Divine Householder, use us in your everyday work, that our faith may not be put back on the shelf or away in the closet. Make our faith evident not only in Sunday worship but also in daily activities at home and elsewhere. Preserve the best of human culture and bring zest to daily life by the presence in the world of your church and its members, young and old, male and female, to the glory of your name. Amen.

PRAYER OF THANKSGIVING
Maker of men and women, Parent of growing children, Teacher for all learners, we give thanks for all whose compassion is shown in more than overflowing emotions, who feed the hungry, find warm beds for weary travelers, carry water for thirsty workers, stop to help the stranded motorist. We praise the generosity of those who

give freely to the poor, who give the shirt off their backs, who loan their cars and machines, who risk what they own on those whose credit is uncertain at best. Your spirit moves them to act as well as speak. You will reward their obedience and ours, as we respond to your prompting. Praise to you, Source of all goodness and love. Amen.

PRAYER OF DEDICATION

What you require of us, God of even-handedness, is not self-denial for its own sake, but caring for the needy; not fasting for a rainy day, but to give food to the hungry. So we give, not that your house should be ornate, but that the light of the Gospel may shine in worship and in public service, like the ministry of Jesus of Nazareth. Amen.

PSALM 112:4-9

Light shines in the darkness for the upright;
The righteous are merciful and full of compassion.
It is good for them to be generous in lending
And to manage their affairs with justice.
For they will never be shaken;
The righteous will be kept in everlasting remembrance.
They will not be afraid of any evil rumors;
Their heart is right; they put their trust in the Lord.
Their heart is established and will not shrink, until they see their
desire upon their enemies.
They have given freely to the poor,
And their righteousness stands fast forever;
And they will hold up their head with honor.

SIXTH SUNDAY AFTER EPIPHANY

Deuteronomy 30:15-20   Psalm 119:1-8
1 Corinthians 3:1-9   Matthew 5:17-26

CALL TO WORSHIP

Choose life. Love, obey, and hold fast to God; that is life for you
and your descendants.

PRAYER OF CONFESSION

*God of all, we confess that we are all too human. We have our
favorites among Christian leaders who sometimes receive the
loyalty that only Christ deserves, and thereby make divisions
among us. We are sometimes jealous of others and strive against
each other instead of working as a team, as your co-workers.
Forgive the immaturity, the unwillingness to rise above the natural
plane, the parochial view that does not fully acknowledge one
holy catholic church and settles for narrow denominationalism.
We need to grow stronger, enabled by the Spirit to rise above
pettiness, to broaden participation in your rule of earth and
heaven, through Jesus Christ, our role model. Amen.*

DECLARATION OF GOD'S FORGIVENESS

Hear the Good News! Whether you are infants in Christ or more
mature, you have the Spirit of God to stimulate your growth.
Friends, believe the Good News! *In Jesus Christ, we are forgiven.*

EXHORTATION

We are God's agents. Let us work as a team and all of us will get
our own pay for our own labor.

PRAYER OF THE DAY

*Heavenly Sovereign, guide and goad us by both law and prophets
to set as our highest priority making peace with our brothers and
sisters, so that we may be properly prepared to offer you our
worship and ready for your just judgment. Amen.*

PRAYER OF THANKSGIVING

*Heavenly Law-giver, Sender of Apostles, Inspirer of prophets, we
give thanks for all whom you have sent to be our guides through
the mazes of decisions that are before us in life. We rejoice in the
diversity we find between Peter and Paul, between Elijah and
Jesus. We celebrate the concerted service of Aquila and Priscilla,
Barnabas and John Mark, and others who, like the twelve, found*

ways of serving you in a variety of combinations. We are grateful for individuals and couples and groups who have shared their faith with us and help us to mature in our understanding of your will and support us in our attempt to do it. With great joy, we remember them all and praise your name with them, an undivided company. Amen.

PRAYER OF DEDICATION

As we offer our gifts, loving God, bring to our minds any unresolved grievance we may have with others, that we may continue the ministry of peacemaking to which we are called as followers of Jesus Christ. Amen.

PSALM 119:1-8

Happy are they whose way is blameless,
Who walk in the law of the Lord!
Happy are they who observe his decrees
And seek him with all their hearts!
Who never do any wrong,
But always walk in his ways.
You laid down your commandments,
That we should fully keep them.
Oh, that my ways were made so direct
That I might keep your statutes!
Then I should not be put to shame,
When I regard all your commandments.
I will thank you with an unfeigned heart,
When I have learned your righteous judgments.
I will keep your statutes;
Do not utterly forsake me.

SEVENTH SUNDAY AFTER EPIPHANY

Isaiah 49:8-13   Psalm 62:5-12
1 Corinthians 3:10-11, 16-23   Matthew 5:27-37

CALL TO WORSHIP
Trust always in God, my people, pour out your hearts before the
One who is our shelter.

PRAYER OF CONFESSION
*Promise-keeping God, we confess that we can make promises
glibly and break them with little regret. We are too easily subject
to our impulses, and slow to bring our desires under the rule of the
mind and the control of your Spirit. Forgive our demands on
others which interfere with their commitments. We are more eager
for others to keep their promises to us than we are to keep
promises more difficult to keep than we had imagined. Forgive us
for breaking our word, through your faithful Son, Jesus Christ our
Savior, who always keeps his promises. Amen.*

DECLARATION OF GOD'S FORGIVENESS
Hear the Good News! Everything belongs to you: the world, life
and death, the present and the future, because you belong to
Christ and Christ to God. Friends, believe the Good News. *In
Jesus Christ, we are forgiven.*

EXHORTATION
Share God's work in putting the land to rights and in caring for
prisoners and others in distress.

PRAYER OF THE DAY
*Stabilize us, good Guide, that we may not falter on the way.
Strengthen our resolves to keep our promises and vows to one
another and to you, that we may be kept in the number of your
covenant people. Make us as good as our word, as you are true to
your promises in Jesus Christ. Amen.*

PRAYER OF THANKSGIVING
*Liberating God, we celebrate the day of deliverance, when you
put the land to rights and share out afresh its desolate fields, when
you set prisoners free, and release them into sunshine and open
air; when you comfort the refugee who travels far to find freedom
and plenty. We rejoice in the sanctuary that we find in you and in
the church founded on Jesus Christ. We are humbly thankful that*

your Spirit dwells in the church, and that there we may gain true
wisdom. All praise be given to you, O God. Amen.

PRAYER OF DEDICATION

God of love and power, we present our offerings and ourselves for
your worship and service, setting our hearts on you and not on
wealth to breed wealth. Use who we are and what we have, for
the eternal church of Jesus Christ. Amen.

PSALM 62:5-12

They bless with their lips,
But in their hearts they curse.
For God alone my soul in silence waits;
Truly, my hope is in him.
He alone is my rock and my salvation,
My stronghold, so that I shall not be shaken.
In God is my safety and my honor;
God is my strong rock and my refuge.
Put your trust in him always, O people,
Pour out your hearts before him, for God is our refuge.
Those of high degree are but a fleeting breath,
Even those of low estate cannot be trusted.
On the scales they are lighter than a breath,
All of them together.
Put no trust in extortion; in robbery take no empty pride;
Though wealth increase, set not your heart upon it.

EIGHTH SUNDAY AFTER EPIPHANY

Leviticus 19:1-2, 9-18   Psalm 119:33-40
1 Corinthians 4:1-5   Matthew 5:38-48

CALL TO WORSHIP
Trust always in God, my people, pour out your hearts before the one who is our shelter.

PRAYER OF CONFESSION
Patient Parent, holy and forgiving, we would rather speak to those who speak to us, to love those who love us in return. We enjoy the common enthusiasms of our own country and its people. We would rather hate our enemies than pray for them and for those who harass us. The passive resistance that Jesus teaches seems unworkable to us and unfair, giving the advantage to our adversaries at the expense of our personal rights. Forgive us for following our own desires and not obeying the instruction of Jesus Christ. Amen.

DECLARATION OF GOD'S FORGIVENESS
Hear the Good News! Our heavenly Parent's goodness knows no bounds. Friends, believe the Good News! *In Jesus Christ, we are forgiven.*

EXHORTATION
Love your neighbor and your enemy, who are persons like yourself. This is God's command.

PRAYER OF THE DAY
Your goodness, O God, knows no bounds. Increase our goodness beyond its present limits to higher stages of maturity, that our love and forgiveness may become more nearly like that of your Son, our Savior, Jesus Christ. Amen.

PRAYER OF THANKSGIVING
Gracious God, your benevolence is not limited to the deserving, or who would receive the many benefits that we take for granted? You make your sun to rise on good and bad alike, and send the rain on the honest and the dishonest. We are grateful for all your gifts and for the friendships that have come to us without our seeking them, for those who have been kind and helpful to us without any initiative on our part. Help us to show our thankfulness by taking the initiative in reaching out to others who

need friends, by going the extra mile to be helpful, especially for
those who may not be able to ask for help. We appreciate being
part of your family gathered in the Spirit. We are humbled by the
thought that as we belong to Christ, we belong to you, God of all.
Amen.

PRAYER OF DEDICATION

You honor us, divine Spirit, by making your home within us. Make
us more fitting temples for your habitation, urging us toward the
maturity and open-heartedness that is the genius of our divine
Parent. Bless our church as a means to that end; through Jesus
Christ our Lord. Amen.

PSALM 119:33-40

Teach me, O Lord, the way of your statutes,
And I shall keep it to the end.
Give me understanding, and I shall keep your law;
I shall keep it with all my heart.
Make me go in the path of your commandments,
For that is my desire.
Incline my heart to your decrees
And not to unjust gain.
Turn my eyes from watching what is worthless;
Give me life in your ways.
Fulfill your promise to your servant,
Which you make to those who fear you.
Turn away the reproach which I dread,
Because your judgments are good.
Behold, I long for your commandments;
In your righteousness preserve my life.

LAST SUNDAY AFTER EPIPHANY
Transfiguration

Exodus 24:12-18   Psalm 2:6-11
2 Peter 1:16-21   Matthew 17:1-9

CALL TO WORSHIP
You will do well to attend to the message of the prophets, because it is like a lamp shining in a murky place, until the day breaks and the morning star rises to illuminate your minds.

PRAYER OF CONFESSION
Majestic God, transfigured Christ, impelling Spirit, we confess that we do not frequent the place of deep silence where the voice of the sublime presence can be heard. Our minds dwell too much on lesser human figures than on your beloved Child, Jesus. Our reading of the prophets takes us too often to the familiar and avoids the difficult and the demanding. Forgive us if we have resisted the leading of the Spirit and missed further illumination that the Spirit can bring; through Jesus Christ, your Favorite. Amen.

DECLARATION OF GOD'S FORGIVENESS
Hear the Good News! The apostles share with us their experience of the coming of our Lord Jesus Christ when he was invested with honor and glory from the sublime Presence. Friends, believe the Good News. *In Jesus Christ, we are forgiven.*

EXHORTATION
Do not interpret any prophecy of Scripture by yourself. The prophecies were written not by any human whim but by those impelled by the Holy Spirit to communicate to us the words of God.

PRAYER OF THE DAY
Keep us, good Lord, from preoccupation with our sacred history and from the tendency to erect sanctuaries that would delay us from going on to other encounters with you in places of human need. Reveal your glory to us in quiet places of meditation and in noisy places of daily life. Amen.

PRAYER OF THANKSGIVING
Transcendent God, all too soon our experiences of your sublime presence fade when we leave the awesome view of what you have

created, whether in macrocosm or microcosm. We remember such experiences with thanksgiving. We rejoice in the awesomeness of your presence as communicated by the grandeur of architecture or the sweep of great music and art. We are humbly grateful for the sense of belonging, when the Spirit draws us into genuine community with the Christ, and we too are favored and know your love. All thanks be given to you, O God. Amen.

PRAYER OF DEDICATION

We worship you, magnificent God, with sincere reverence, knowing that no gift is worthy of you, but that you graciously receive us and what we bring for the sake of Jesus Christ, your Son, our Lord. Amen.

PSALM 2:6-11

"I myself have set my king upon my holy hill of Zion."
Let me announce the decree of the Lord:
He said to me, "You are my Son;
This day have I begotten you.
Ask of me, and I will give you the nations for your inheritance
And the ends of the earth for your possession.
You shall crush them with an iron rod
And shatter them like a piece of pottery."
And now, you kings, be wise;
Be warned, you rulers of the earth.
Submit to the Lord with fear,
And with trembling bow before him.

ASH WEDNESDAY

Joel 2:12-18   Psalm 51:1-12
2 Corinthians 5:20-6:2   Matthew 6:1-6, 16-18

CALL TO WORSHIP

Rend your hearts and not your garments; turn back to your Sovereign God, who is gracious and compassionate, long-suffering and ever constant.

PRAYER OF CONFESSION

Ever-present Parent, you see what is secret: what others do not see. We cannot hide from you the private charity, the silent prayer, the unannounced fast. We confess that such charities are too few, such prayers too infrequent, such self-denial too rare. We prefer the present rewards of praise and recognition. Forgive worship and service that are insincere, more for appearances than to do your will, through Jesus Christ, ever-faithful. Amen.

DECLARATION OF GOD'S FORGIVENESS

Hear the Good News! You have received the grace of God. The day of deliverance has dawned. Friends, believe the Good News. *In Jesus Christ, we are forgiven.*

EXHORTATION

Share in God's Work. Having received the grace of God, do not waste it.

PRAYER OF THE DAY

Humble Savior, keep us from prideful worship, from parading our good works, from dramatizing our self-denial, so that our love for you, our neighbor and ourselves may be more sincere, and so acknowledged by you in heaven. Amen.

PRAYER OF THANKSGIVING

Patient Parent, you continue to call us back from hypocrisy that shadows true worship, and we are grateful for that. We are thankful also that you allow us to share in your work, even when we spoil it at times by our patronizing airs. We honor the Christ who served you more honestly and humbly, setting an example for us. We appreciate your gracious favor in hearing and heeding our prayers and sending us aid as we need it. We celebrate your love and compassion, helping Holy Spirit. Amen.

PRAYER OF DEDICATION

Without fanfare, O God, we present our offerings and ourselves to share in the work that you continue to do in the world through imperfect human agencies, through the grace of our savior, Jesus Christ. Amen.

PSALM 51:1-12

Have mercy on me, O God, according to your loving-kindness;
In your great compassion blot out my offenses.
Wash me through and through from my wickedness
And cleanse me from my sin.
For I know my transgressions,
And my sin is ever before me.
Against you only have I sinned
And done what is evil in your sight.
And so you are justified when you speak
And upright in your judgment.
Indeed, I have been wicked from my birth,
A sinner from my mother's womb.
For behold, you look for truth deep within me,
And will make me understand wisdom secretly.
Purge me from my sin, and I shall be pure;
Wash me, and I shall be clean indeed.
Make me hear of joy and gladness,
That the body you have broken may rejoice.
Hide your face from my sins
And blot out all my iniquities.
Create in me a clean heart, O God,
And renew a right spirit within me.
Cast me not away from your presence
And take not your holy Spirit from me.

FIRST SUNDAY IN LENT

Genesis 2:4b-9, 15-17, 25; 3:1-7   Psalm 130
Romans 5:12-19   Matthew 4:1-11

CALL TO WORSHIP
O people of God, wait for our heavenly Sovereign; for with our Ruler is mercy; with God there is plenteous redemption, and we shall be redeemed from all our sins.

PRAYER OF CONFESSION
Planter of gardens, Maker of humans, Shaper of minds, we confess that we would be like gods, knowing what is good and what is bad. We would like to make our own rules to live by, and frequently do, but we cannot always escape the nagging sense of guilt, even when we have determined that our new rules are better than the old. Forgive us for living below the best we know; for projecting better behavior that would improve our human condition, but being unwilling to change even some of our simpler habits of daily life. Replace our guilt with energy to reform ourselves, with reshaping by the Spirit of Jesus Christ. Amen.

DECLARATION OF GOD'S FORGIVENESS
Hear the Good News! Just as through human disobedience all became sinners, so through Jesus Christ, all shall become just. Friends, believe the Good News! *In Jesus Christ, we are forgiven.*

EXHORTATION
Receive the overflowing grace, the gift of justice, that you may live and reign through the one key person, Jesus Christ.

PRAYER OF THE DAY
Spirit of God, lead us safely through the temptation to live primarily for the satisfaction of bodily needs. Save us from presuming on your care at the other extreme and being careless with the life that is precious in the sight of the Creator. Preserve us from adulation of any human being, however attractive and powerful, that we may worship faithfully God in Jesus Christ. Amen.

PRAYER OF THANKSGIVING
How generous you are, eternal and timely Giver! You give us a great abundance of life, human, animal, vegetable. You give us

puzzles to solve with our minds. You give us beauty to admire, and inspire our artistry. You entertain us with cunning animals. You face us with moral dilemmas and graciously forgive our failures to live by the best choice. You give us opportunity for adventuring in the world, to prepare us for the privilege of living with Christ in the world that is coming, where you are undisputed Ruler. With angels and all your creation we will give homage to you, then and now. Amen.

PRAYER OF DEDICATION
Nothing that we give you was made by us from nothing, but is our reshaping or using what you have already created. Magnificent and merciful Creator, receive our gifts, rude and simple as they may be, but given from thankful hearts and hands. Amen.

PSALM 130
Out of the depths have I called to you, O Lord; Lord, hear my
   voice;
Let your ears consider well the voice of my supplication.
If you, Lord, were to note what is done amiss, O Lord, who could
   stand?
For there is forgiveness with you; therefore you shall be feared.
I will wait for the Lord; my soul waits for him;
In his word is my hope.
My soul waits for the Lord, more than watchmen for the morning,
More than watchmen for the morning.
O Israel, wait for the Lord, for with the Lord there is mercy;
*With him there is plenteous redemption, and he shall redeem
   Israel from all their sins.*

SECOND SUNDAY IN LENT

Genesis 12:1-8   Psalm 33:18-22
Romans 4:1-5, 13-16a   John 3:1-7
                                                      (Matthew 17:1-9)

CALL TO WORSHIP
Wait eagerly for the One who comes, who is our help and our
shield. The eye of God is upon all who wait upon his love.

PRAYER OF CONFESSION
*World-loving Creator, Son-giving Parent, life-giving Spirit, we
confess our disbelief in the face of mysteries that we cannot
explain. We fear and resist spiritual transformation as if you
would change us beyond our own recognition. Though we cannot
control the winds, we would attempt to program the Spirit.
Forgive our doubts concerning your love and our restrictions on
your purpose for us in Jesus Christ. Amen.*

DECLARATION OF GOD'S FORGIVENESS
Hear the Good News! Our faith in God, like Abraham's, is
counted as righteousness, a matter of sheer grace. Friends,
believe the Good News. *In Jesus Christ, we are forgiven.*

EXHORTATION
Do not be afraid of new experiences of God. Be enabled by them
to go on as a more faithful disciple of Jesus Christ.

PRAYER OF THANKSGIVING
*God of pilgrims, we rejoice in your presence with your people.
You have led our fathers and mothers on journeys out of idolatry,
slavery, and religious oppression, to places of new insights, to
times of further reformation, on missions of truth-sharing. We give
thanks for the heritage of faith that is ours and for the riches of
grace that are ours in Christ Jesus. As we share this heritage in our
generation, bless all the families of the earth as you have blessed
us, in the name of Jesus Christ. Amen.*

PRAYER OF DEDICATION
*Not only in this sanctuary, but wherever we meet you in our
experience, receive our offering of ourselves, God-above-all, that
we may build altars and serve others to honor your name. Amen.*

PSALM 33:18-22

Behold, the eye of the Lord is upon those who fear him,
On those who wait upon his love,
To pluck their lives from death,
And to feed them in time of famine.
Our soul waits for the Lord;
He is our help and our shield.
Indeed, our heart rejoices in him,
For in his holy Name we put our trust.
Let your loving-kindness, O Lord, be upon us,
As we have put our trust in you.

THIRD SUNDAY IN LENT

Exodus 17:3-7

Romans 5:1-5

Psalm 95

John 4:5-26

CALL TO WORSHIP

By the power of God's Spirit, worship the Eternal who really is, offering God the true worship that is wanted.

PRAYER OF CONFESSION

God of all nations, forgive our biases and prejudices, our refusal to have dealings with those of other races and orientations of which we do not approve. Excuse our religious one-upmanship that seeks to exalt our own persuasion at the expense of others, and that would rather debate non-essentials than find common ground and concerted action. We are convinced that we are right, and stubborn in resisting any evidence that we should change our minds. Soften such hardness of heart with the warm love of the Spirit; through Jesus Christ our Lord. Amen.

DECLARATION OF GOD'S FORGIVENESS

Hear the Good News! We have been put right with God through faith; we have peace with God through our Lord Jesus Christ. Friends, believe the Good News. *In Jesus Christ, we are forgiven.*

EXHORTATION

Don't be stubborn. Listen today to what God says. Do not refuse to obey what God commands and miss the fulfillment of the promises made for us in Christ.

PRAYER OF THE DAY

Well-spring of eternal life, satisfy our thirst for life today and every day along life's journey through wilderness ways. Help us to find time, in these forty days and nights of Lent, and on all of our days, for spiritual refreshment and growth in grace, your grace, Lord Jesus Christ. Amen.

PRAYER OF THANKSGIVING

God our Maker and Re-Maker, we sing for joy to you, for you care for us and provide for us. You accept us despite our history of failures. By faith, we experience your grace and the renewal of our relationship with you in Christ. We find it difficult to rejoice in our troubles, but we do rejoice in the endurance and the hope which your approval brings. Above all, we give thanks for the gift of your Holy Spirit filling us with love for you, and the hope of sharing your glory. Amen.

PRAYER OF DEDICATION

For generations you have been worshiped in this place, God of our ancestors, Father of our Lord Jesus Christ. Whenever and wherever your children come to you, receive their offering of true worship through the universal Spirit. Amen.

PSALM 95

Come, let us sing to the Lord;
Let us shout joy to the Rock of our salvation.
Let us come before his presence with thanksgiving
And raise a loud shout to him with psalms.
For the Lord is a great God,
And a great King above all gods.
In his hand are the caverns of the earth,
And the heights of the hills are his also.
The sea is his, for he made it,
And his hands have molded the dry land.
Come, let us bow down, and bend the knee,
And kneel before the Lord our Maker.
For he is our God,
And we are the people of his pasture and the sheep of his hand.
Oh, that today you would hearken to his voice!
Harden not your hearts, as your forebears did in the wilderness, at
    Meribah,
And on that day at Massah, when they tempted me.
They put me to the test, though they had seen my works.
Forty years long I detested that generation and said, "This people
    are wayward in their hearts; they do not know my ways."
So I swore in my wrath, "They shall not enter into my rest."

FOURTH SUNDAY IN LENT

1 Samuel 16:1-13   Psalm 23
Ephesians 5:8-14   John 9:1-41

CALL TO WORSHIP

Christ is the light of the world. As Christians you are light and
should leave darkness behind. Live like those who feel at home in
daylight.

PRAYER OF CONFESSION

*One true Judge, you know us better than we know ourselves. You
know our hearts and our thoughts, our motives as well as our
actions. We confess that we tend to judge others and ourselves
too much by appearances, by physical graces rather than spiritual
graces, by traditional manners rather than spontaneous
helpfulness, by announced intentions rather than actual behavior.
We would dread your true judgment, except for the mercy and
goodness you offer us in Jesus Christ. Amen.*

DECLARATION OF GOD'S FORGIVENESS

Hear the Good News! Though you once were all darkness, now as
Christians you are light. Friends, believe the Good News. *In Jesus
Christ, we are forgiven.*

EXHORTATION

Live like those who are at home in the light, for where the light is,
there all goodness springs up, all justice and truth.

PRAYER OF THE DAY

*Light Source, Light of our eyes, Light of our souls, open our eyes
that we may see things clearly and honestly, making judgments as
you make them and turning from all darkness, live in the light of
truth and goodness and justice for all. Amen.*

PRAYER OF THANKSGIVING

*Generous Provider, you pour out such great blessings that our cup
runs over. Anointing Spirit, you touch us with the oil of gladness
and make our faces shine with joy. Heaven-sent Healer, you do
God's work with great simplicity, healing our sicknesses and
restoring our souls. We give thanks to you and worship you with
slowly-deepening appreciation. Glory be to you, Light-above-us,
Light-of-the-world, Light-within-us. Amen.*

PRAYER OF DEDICATION

Divine Sovereign, elector and rejector of earthly authorities, only the Holy Spirit can hallow us to appear before you, and only the Spirit enables us to perform any service worthy of offering to you. Receive what we offer for the sake of great David's greater Son, even Jesus Christ. Amen.

PSALM 23

The Lord is my shepherd;
I shall not be in want.
He makes me lie down in green pastures
And leads me beside still waters.
He revives my soul and guides me along right pathways for his
    Name's sake.
*Though I walk through the valley of the shadow of death, I shall
    fear no evil;*
For you are with me;
Your rod and your staff, they comfort me.
You spread a table before me in the presence of those who
    trouble me;
You have anointed my head with oil, and my cup is running over.
Surely your goodness and mercy shall follow me all the days of
    my life,
And I will dwell in the house of the Lord for ever.

FIFTH SUNDAY IN LENT

Ezekiel 37:1-14   Psalm 116:1-9
Romans 8:6-11   John 11:(1-16) 17-45

CALL TO WORSHIP
Open your heart to the Spirit of hope, like someone in the darkness looking for the first light of dawn.

PRAYER OF CONFESSION
God of our yesterdays, our today, and our tomorrows, we are too prone to live for the moment, to let our health and our emotions and our passions rule our lives. You offer us the Spirit to bring these things into wholeness under your control, but we resist and often are overtaken by events, and sink into despair. From the depths you would raise us if we cry out to you, but at times it seems we prefer sullen silence. Forgive self-pity that closes you out. We pray in the name of Jesus Christ. Amen.

DECLARATION OF GOD'S FORGIVENESS
Hear the Good News! In the Lord is love unfailing, and great is his power to set us free. God alone sets us free from all our sins. Friends, believe the Good News. *In Jesus Christ, we are forgiven.*

EXHORTATION
Live on the level of the spirit. Keep the spiritual outlook that is life and peace.

PRAYER OF THE DAY
Loose us, living Lord, from the fear of death and its power, to live freely the life of the spirit, in obedience to your command, so that, invigorated by the indwelling Spirit, we may accomplish your purposes, to the glory of your name. Amen.

PRAYER OF THANKSGIVING
Living God, untouched by death; incarnate Son of God, Conqueror of death; life-giving Spirit of God; we tax our minds and our language to praise you, even to name you. No thanksgiving we offer is adequate. Human life is a mystery: your life even more so. Your love for us mortals, like the love of Jesus for Lazarus, defies description. We find unending joy in the assurance of your love and the promise of eternal life with you and with all whom we love. Amen.

PRAYER OF DEDICATION

These offerings, good Lord, are life-giving only as your Spirit enables us as the church to do your work in the world. Bless and use us in your service of others. Amen.

PSALM 116:1-9

I love the Lord, because he has heard the voice of my supplication,
Because he has inclined his ear to me whenever I called upon him.
The cords of death entangled me;
The grip of the grave took hold of me; I came to grief and sorrow.
Then I called upon the Name of the Lord:
"O Lord, I pray you, save my life."
Gracious is the Lord and righteous:
Our God is full of compassion.
The Lord watches over the innocent;
I was brought very low, and he helped me.
Turn again to your rest, O my soul,
For the Lord has treated you well.
For you have rescued my life from death,
My eyes from tears, and my feet from stumbling.
I will walk in the presence of the Lord in the land of the living.
I believed, even when I said, "I have been brought very low."

SIXTH SUNDAY IN LENT
When Observed as PASSION SUNDAY

Isaiah 50:4-9a   Psalm 31:9-16
Philippians 2:5-11   (Matthew 26:14-17; 66)
                                                 Matthew 27:11-54

CALL TO WORSHIP
Glorify God, bow your knee at the name of Jesus, and confess
that "Jesus Christ is Lord."

PRAYER OF CONFESSION
*Court of last appeal, we are too ready to judge others and to
defend ourselves. We are impatient that you should set things
right and vindicate our "good name." We are more prone to insult
others than to accept slight and insult with patience. Rather than
turn the other cheek, we lash out with as much vehemence as we
can gather. Rather than keep silence, we resort to name-calling
and other verbal abuse. Forgive our short tempers and abuse of
others, for the sake of the forbearing Christ. Amen.*

DECLARATION OF GOD'S FORGIVENESS
Hear the Good News! The divine Child came in humility, as a
human, to the lowliness of servanthood and the shame of a
criminal's death, and for his obedience, God raised him to the
heights and bestowed on him the Name above all names. Friends,
believe the Good News! *In Jesus Christ, we are forgiven.*

EXHORTATION
Let your bearing toward one another arise out of your life in
Christ Jesus.

PRAYER OF THE DAY
*Divine Parent, whenever we think life is unfair to us or that we are
given more than our share of suffering, remind us of the patience
of Jesus and his trust, despite feelings of abandonment, so that our
faith will not fail and our trust in you give evidence that we also
are your children. Amen.*

PRAYER OF THANKSGIVING
*God of glory, God of grace, we rejoice with humble hearts as we
celebrate the condescension of the One who was your equal, but
left such glory for a while, to become human, in the lowliness of
servitude, the pain of suffering and the indignity of death. We*

raise our voices to praise the recognition that you give the Christ again, in raising him to the heights and bestowing on him the supreme Name in the whole universe, announcing that Jesus the anointed is Lord. All glory be given to you, in praise of your vulnerability and your victory, one God, great in grace and great in glory. Amen.

PRAYER OF DEDICATION

No offering that we bring can compare, O God, with the offering of your Son Jesus, and the self-offering that he makes on the cross. Nevertheless, may that example move us beyond giving to the genuine offering of ourselves in obedient service at all costs, for Jesus' sake. Amen.

PSALM 31:9-16

Have mercy on me, O Lord, for I am in trouble;
My eye is consumed with sorrow, and also my throat and my belly.
For my life is wasted with grief, and my years with sighing;
My strength fails me because of affliction, and my bones are consumed.
I have become a reproach to all my enemies and even to my neighbors,
A dismay to those of my acquaintance; when they see me in the street they avoid me.
I am forgotten like a dead man, out of mind;
I am as useless as a broken pot.
For I have heard the whispering of the crowd; fear is all around,
They put their heads together against me; they plot to take my life.
But as for me, I have trusted in you, O Lord.
I have said, "You are my God.
My times are in your hand;
Rescue me from the hand of my enemies, and from those who persecute me.
Make your face to shine upon your servant,
And in your loving-kindness save me."

SIXTH SUNDAY IN LENT
When celebrated as PALM SUNDAY

Isaiah 50:4-9a   Psalm 118:19-29
Philippians 2:5-11   Matthew 21:1-11
                                                  (John 12:12-16)

CALL TO WORSHIP
Glorify God, bow your knee at the name of Jesus, and confess
that "Jesus Christ is Lord."

PRAYER OF CONFESSION
*Court of last appeal, we are too ready to judge others and to
defend ourselves. We are impatient that you should set things
right and vindicate our "good name." We are more prone to insult
others than to accept slight and insult with patience. Rather than
turn the other cheek, we lash out with as much vehemence as we
can gather. Rather than keep silence, we resort to name-calling
and other verbal abuse. Forgive our short tempers and abuse of
others, for the sake of the forbearing Christ. Amen.*

DECLARATION OF GOD'S FORGIVENESS
Hear the Good News! The divine Child came in humility, as a
human, to the lowliness of servanthood and the shame of a
criminal's death, and for his obedience, God raised him to the
heights and bestowed on him the Name above all names. Friends,
believe the Good News! *In Jesus Christ, we are forgiven.*

EXHORTATION
Let your bearing toward one another arise out of your life in
Christ Jesus.

PRAYER OF THE DAY
*Sovereign Jesus, after the excitement of the parade has passed,
grant us pause to meditate on the majesty of your gentleness and
the truth of what you teach and what you are, for we would
become more like you as bearers of the name, Christian. Amen.*

PRAYER OF THANKSGIVING
*God of glory, god of Grace, we rejoice with humble hearts as we
celebrate the condescension of the One who was your equal, but
left such glory for a while, to become human, in the lowliness of
servitude, the pain of suffering and the indignity of death. We
raise our voices to praise the recognition that you give the Christ*

again in raising him to the heights and bestowing on him the supreme Name in the whole universe, announcing that Jesus the anointed is Lord. All glory be given to you, in praise of your vulnerability and your victory, one God, great in grace and great in glory. Amen.

PRAYER OF DEDICATION

No offering that we bring can compare, O God, with the offering of your Son Jesus, and the self-offering that he makes on the cross. Nevertheless, may that example move us beyond giving to the genuine offering of ourselves in obedient service at all costs, for Jesus' sake. Amen.

PSALM 118:19-29

Open for me the gates of righteousness; I will enter them; I will offer thanks to the Lord.
"This is the gate of the Lord; he who is righteous may enter."
I will give thanks to you, for you answered me and have become my salvation.
The same stone which the builders rejected has become the chief cornerstone.
This is the Lord's doing, and it is marvelous in our eyes.
On this day the Lord has acted; we will rejoice and be glad in it.
Hosannah, Lord, hosannah!
Lord, send us now success.
Blessed is he who comes in the name of the Lord;
We bless you from the house of the Lord.
God is the Lord; he has shined upon us;
Form a procession with branches up to the horns of the altar.
"You are my God, and I will thank you;
You are my God, and I will exalt you."
Give thanks to the Lord, for he is good;
His mercy endures for ever.

MAUNDY THURSDAY

The Matthew Passion Narrative Divided into Eleven Lessons for a Tenebrae Service with Holy Communion or the Last Supper and some suggested hymns

Matthew 21:12-17 Temple Echoes of the Entry Into Jerusalem
           Hymn: Hosanna, Loud Hosanna, verse one
21:18-27 The Restrained Power to Destroy
           Hymn: Fairest Lord Jesus, Ruler of All Nature, verse one
23:29-24:8 Challenge to Jerusalem
26:1-16 The Scheme of Arrest
           Hymn: O Come and Mourn with Me Awhile
           (first verse)
26:17-30 The Last Supper
           Hymn: 'Twas on That Night When Doomed to Know

HOLY COMMUNION

26:30-56 Gethsemane
           Hymn: Go to Dark Gethsemane
26:57-75 The House of Caiaphas
           Hymn: In the Hour of Trial
27:1-10 The Blood Money
           Hymn: Ah, Dearest Jesus, How Hast Thou Offended
27:11-31 The Trial and Humiliation
           Hymn: There Is a Green Hill Far Away
27:32-54 The Crucifixion
           Hymn: O Sacred Head Now Wounded
27:55-66 The Arrangements and the Burial

A flame-shaped mark may be made in the margin of the text of Scripture as a cue for the gradual extinction of seven candles, one at a time.

1. His Death Is Schemed — 26:3
2. The Betrayal Is Acknowledged — 26:24
3. The Arrest in the Night and the Desertion of the Disciples — 26:56
4. Abuse at the House of the High Priest — 26:67
5. Peter Disowns Christ — 26:75
6. Christ Rather than the Crook Is Condemned — 27:23
7. The Darkness of Crucifixion — 27:45

EASTER

Acts 10:34-43
(Jeremiah 31:1-6)
Colossians 3:1-4

Psalm 118:14-24
John 20:1-9
(Matthew 28:1-10)

CALL TO WORSHIP
This is the day on which our Lord has acted: Let us exult and rejoice in it.

PRAYER OF CONFESSION
God of heaven and earth, God of flesh and spirit, Spirit of God and of the church, the world is too much with us; late and soon, getting and spending, we lay waste our powers, but it is not so much the harmony with nature that we have lost, but our accord with heaven. What we excuse as merely human, you have condemned as sinful. We squirm at the description of our faults by prophets and apostles, not prepared to abandon our old ways, because we have not lifted our eyes beyond the present state of things to the realm above and to the eternity beyond death. Forgive our lack of vision and spiritual aspiration, for the sake of your Son, Jesus Christ. Amen.

DECLARATION OF GOD'S FORGIVENESS
Hear the Good News! Jesus Christ is the one who has been designated by God as Judge of the living and the dead. It is to him that all the prophets testify, declaring that everyone who trusts in him receives forgiveness of sins through his name. Friends, believe the Good News. *In Jesus Christ, we are forgiven.*

EXHORTATION
Aspire to the realm above, where Christ is, seated at the right hand of God, and let your thoughts dwell on that higher realm, not on this earthly life. Now your life lies hidden with Christ in God. When Christ, who is our life, is manifested, then you too will be manifested with him in glory.

PRAYER OF THE DAY
Living God, dying and rising Christ, life-giving Spirit, save us from our doubts and fears. Enrich our lives with a growing knowledge of the Scriptures, so that the unfolding story of our life and death may bring new understanding of your word in wisdom, for living and sharing with others on our way. Amen.

PRAYER OF THANKSGIVING

It is good to give thanks to you, O Lord,
    For your love endures forever.
We declare it with the House of Israel,
    For your love endures forever.
We declare it with the church of the risen Christ,
    For your love endures forever.
We declare it with seeking disciples,
    For your love endures forever.
We declare it with the bereaved and the dying,
    For your love endures forever,
In Jesus Christ, crucified, and risen. Amen.

PRAYER OF DEDICATION

Miracle-working God: what others reject as useless, you accept and utilize. We give ourselves and our offerings, in the confidence that you will make valuable what might have been wasted; through Jesus Christ, who is alive and with you, and through the Spirit who is with us. Amen.

PSALM 118:14-24

The Lord is my strength and my song,
And he has become my salvation.
There is a sound of exultation and victory in the tents of the
    righteous:
"The right hand of the Lord has triumphed!
The right hand of the Lord is exalted!
The right hand of the Lord has triumphed!"
I shall not die, but live, and declare the works of the Lord.
The Lord has punished me sorely, but he did not hand me over to
    death.
Open for me the gates of righteousness; I will enter them; I will
    offer thanks to the Lord.
"This is the gate of the Lord; he who is righteous may enter."
I will give thanks to you, for you answered me and have become
    my salvation.
The same stone which the builders rejected has become the chief
    cornerstone.
This is the Lord's doing, and it is marvelous in our eyes.
On this day the Lord has acted; we will rejoice and be glad in it.

SECOND SUNDAY OF EASTER

Acts 2:14a, 22-32
1 Peter 1:3-9

Psalm 16:5-11
(John 20:19-31)
Matthew 28:11-20

CALL TO WORSHIP
Bless our God who has given us counsel. Come to worship with exulting heart and rejoicing spirit.

PRAYER OF CONFESSION
God of creation and resurrection, Savior by birth, death and resurrection, Spirit of our rebirth into hope, we confess that we can take our hope for granted. The passing of Easter year after year is accepted in many ways as routine, and we forget that the first Easter is unique in human history. If we give short shrift to the significance of the resurrection of Jesus, forgive such indifference. The death of a loved one or the imminence of our own death will test our faith soon enough, and we need a strong faith to sustain us; in the living Lord. Amen.

DECLARATION OF GOD'S FORGIVENESS
Hear the Good News! God, with great mercy, has given us a new birth into a living hope, through the resurrection of Jesus Christ from the dead. Friends, believe the Good News. *In Jesus Christ, we are forgiven.*

FILED

EXHORTATION
Trust the Christ you cannot see and love him with joy beyond words, for that faith brings at last the salvation of your soul.

PRAYER OF THE DAY
Paternal, fraternal, maternal God, we have received your names at our baptism, as Father, Son and Holy Spirit. Empower us to make all nations your disciples, teaching them to observe all that you have commanded, so that they too may worship you and know your presence to the end of time. Amen.

PRAYER OF THANKSGIVING
God of purpose, portents and plans, no rebel power can defeat your final purposes, and we look for continuing signs that your objectives will be realized. In Jesus of Nazareth, you fulfill ancient promises to David, not with earthly pomp and circumstance, but with heavenly power over death, through

62

resurrection. No ancient throne can bring us gladness, but the presence of the living Christ through the Spirit brings us joy and hope of eternal life. We are filled with thanksgiving in the confidence that you do not abandon us in death, but lead us on in the way of life. All glory be given to you, O God. Amen.

PRAYER OF DEDICATION
Sovereign God, though you can accomplish your purposes despite the wicked and the evil use of money, we would rather be among your disciples, serving you knowingly with what we have and what we are, in obedient faith. Amen.

PSALM 16:5-11
O Lord, you are my portion and my cup;
It is you who uphold my lot.
My boundaries enclose a pleasant land;
Indeed, I have a goodly heritage.
I will bless the Lord who gives me counsel;
My heart teaches me, night after night.
I have set the Lord always before me;
Because he is at my right hand I shall not fall.
My heart, therefore, is glad, and my spirit rejoices;
My body also shall rest in hope.
For you will not abandon me to the grave,
Nor let your holy one see the Pit.
You will show me the path of life;
*And in your presence there is fullness of joy, and in your right
     hand are pleasures for evermore.*

THIRD SUNDAY OF EASTER

Acts 2:14a, 36-41   Psalm 116:12-19
1 Peter 1:17-21   Luke 24:13-35

CALL TO WORSHIP
Repent and be baptized, every one of you, in the name of Jesus
the Messiah, for the forgiveness of your sins; and you will receive
the gift of the Holy Spirit. For the promise is to you and to your
children and to all who are far away, everyone whom the Lord
our God may call.

PRAYER OF CONFESSION
*Truthful God, patient Teacher, Inspiration of prophets, we confess
that we are often dull and sluggish in our thinking, and slow of
heart in believing. We prefer to hear what we already know than to
think out something we have not heard before. We cherish our
mixture of faith and doubt, rather than seek the surer faith that
comes with a broader knowledge of the Scriptures. Forgive our
use of less than our full intellectual capacities in worship, and less
than an adventurous faith in following you; through Jesus Christ,
fully human, fully divine. Amen.*

DECLARATION OF GOD'S FORGIVENESS
Hear the Good News! It was no perishable stuff, like gold or
silver, that bought your freedom from the empty folly of your
traditional ways. The price was paid in precious blood, as it were
of a lamb without mark or blemish — the blood of Christ.
Friends, believe the Good News! *In Jesus Christ, we are forgiven.*

EXHORTATION
Fix your faith and hope in God, who raised Christ from the dead
and gave him glory, the One who judges everyone impartially on
the record of his deeds.

PRAYER OF THE DAY
*Make yourself known to us again, risen Lord, in the breaking of the
bread, so that every gathering of your people around your table
may be a confirmation of the Good News that you are alive from
the dead, and accompanying your people in the events of their
journey. Amen.*

PRAYER OF THANKSGIVING
To know you, O God, is our joy. To be released from bondage to

64

lesser "gods" is to be free to enjoy you anywhere and anytime. Our hearts exult in your love. Our spirits rejoice in communion with you. Our bodies are restful in the absence of fear when we remember your power over death. You lead us in the path of life. Your immediate presence will be fullness of joy. The honor you give is more pleasurable than earth's greatest tributes. Thanks are given to you, heavenly Parent, for giving the heavenly Son to the earthly death of the cross. Thanks are given to you, death-defying God, for raising Jesus of Nazareth from the dead, to prove that death could not keep him in its grip. Thanks are given to you, eternal Spirit, for inspiring our hope and our trust in you. Amen.

PRAYER OF DEDICATION

Crucified Jesus and risen Christ, your gift of baptism as a sacrament in the church makes simple washing with water the sign of forgiveness to the repentant, and a gesture of acceptance to our children. Use us and our offerings to maintain the church and all your means of grace, in the holy names of God. Amen.

PSALM 116:12-19

I will fulfill my vows to the Lord in the presence of all his people.
Precious in the sight of the Lord is the death of his servants.
O Lord, I am your servant;
I am your servant and the child of your handmaid; you have freed me from my bonds.
I will offer you the sacrifice of thanksgiving
And call upon the Name of the Lord.
I will fulfill my vows to the Lord in the presence of all his people,
In the courts of the Lord's house, in the midst of you,
O Jerusalem, Hallelujah!

FOURTH SUNDAY IN EASTER

Acts 2:42-47   Psalm 23
1 Peter 2:19-25   John 10:1-10

CALL TO WORSHIP

Hear the word of Jesus: I have come that you may have life and
that you may have it in all its fullness. I am the door; anyone who
comes into the fold through me shall be safe.

PRAYER OF CONFESSION

*Shepherd-God, who creates the fold; Shepherd-God, who goes out
to seek the lost sheep; Shepherd-God, who draws the flock
together; we have strayed like sheep and though you have brought
us to your fold, we have not always followed in your steps. We
may have begun to live the good life, but turn back too often to
the old, sinful life. We acknowledge the example Christ has set for
us, but too rarely accept the promised gifts of the Spirit to be like
him. Forgive our wandering ways and grant us repentance and
forgiveness for the sake of Jesus Christ, who suffered on our
behalf. Amen.*

DECLARATION OF GOD'S FORGIVENESS

Hear the Good News! In his own person, Jesus carried our sins to
the cross. By his wounds we are healed. Friends, believe the
Good News! *In Jesus Christ, we are forgiven.*

EXHORTATION

Repent and be baptized, everyone of you, in the name of Jesus
the Messiah, for the forgiveness of sins; and you will receive the
gift of the Holy Spirit. For the promise is to you and to your
children and to all who are far away, everyone whom the Lord
our God may call.

PRAYER OF THE DAY

*Shepherd and Guardian of our souls, keep on calling us by name,
so that we may not turn aside to follow the voice of anyone else
who would destroy our faith and impoverish our life. Grant us
fullness of life in your goodness and love unfailing. Amen.*

PRAYER OF THANKSGIVING

*Good Shepherd, we rejoice in the bounteous provision you make
for us so that we want nothing. We rest in the pleasant places life
affords and in the peaceful times. We are thankful for the renewal*

of our life and strength. After struggle and weariness. Even
when life is dark and the shadow of death falls on us or
those we love, you give us comfort and hope. When adversity
closes us in, you send us surprises that fill our cup to overflowing.
Your goodness and unfailing love will keep us in your household
all the days of our lives, filled with praise and prayer. Amen.

PRAYER OF DEDICATION

Divine Doorkeeper, receive our gifts and the witness of our words
and lives, not only to keep these church doors open for us and our
families, but to all whom you shall call into the company of faith
and add to our number by baptism in the name of the Father, the
Son and the Holy Spirit. Amen.

PSALM 23

The Lord is my shepherd;
I shall not be in want.
He makes me lie down in green pastures
And leads me beside still waters.
He revives my soul and guides me along right pathways for his
 Name's sake.
*Though I walk through the valley of the shadow of death, I shall
 fear no evil;*
For you are with me;
Your rod and your staff, they comfort me.
You spread a table before me in the presence of those who
 trouble me;
You have anointed my head with oil, and my cup is running over.
Surely your goodness and mercy shall follow me all the days of
 my life,
And I will dwell in the house of the Lord forever.

FIFTH SUNDAY OF EASTER

Acts 7:55-60   Psalm 31:1-8
1 Peter 2:2-10   John 14:1-14

CALL TO WORSHIP
Come to the Lord, our living Stone — the Stone rejected by many
but choice and precious in the sight of God. Come, and let
yourselves be built as living stones into a spiritual temple;
become a holy priesthood, to offer spiritual sacrifices
acceptable to God through Jesus Christ.

PRAYER OF CONFESSION
*Invisible Father, seen only in the visible Son, invisible Worker at
work in Jesus of Nazareth, divine Doer doing greater things still in
those who have faith in you; forgive our failure to accomplish
what you have wanted to do through us. Too often we have
allowed our faith to grow weak, not sustaining it with honest
questions addressed to you in your church and in your word.
Like Thomas and Philip, we have had doubts or a lack of
understanding, but not the same readiness to get our questions
answered. Forgive our wandering, our fuzzymindedness, our lack
of vitality, when you have given us Jesus to be for us the way, the
truth and the life. Amen.*

DECLARATION OF GOD'S FORGIVENESS
Hear the Good News! You are now the people of God, who once
were not; once outside God's mercy, now you have received
mercy. Friends, believe the Good News. *In Jesus Christ, we are
forgiven.*

EXHORTATION
You are a people owned by God, to proclaim the triumphs of
Christ, who has called you out of darkness into marvelous light.

PRAYER OF THE DAY
*Bring us to your house, heavenly Parent, trusting in your
preparation to receive us, following Jesus who is the way, learning
of Jesus who is the truth, drawing strength from Jesus who is the
life. Amen.*

PRAYER OF THANKSGIVING
*Light in darkness, Life out of death, Creator of unity, we rejoice in
the triumphs of your love and grace. Out of darkness and doubt*

68

and distress you bring us to light and certainty and peace. Out of mortality and fear of death and unbelief, you lead us to trust and hope and eternal life. Out of scatteredness and shapelessness and clumsy purposelessness, you make us into a people, a worshiping community, a corporation for service; through Jesus Christ, Prince of priests. Amen.

PRAYER OF DEDICATION

Creator and Sustainer of the church, so keep us in the faith that we may not be separated from you and one another, but united in a common service with diverse but complementary gifts to offer you, through Jesus Christ. Amen.

PSALM 31:1-8

In you, O Lord, have I taken refuge; let me never be put to shame;
Deliver me in your righteousness.
Incline your ear to me;
Make haste to deliver me.
Be my strong rock, a castle to keep me safe,
For you are my crag and my stronghold;
For the sake of your Name, lead me and guide me.
Take me out of the net that they have secretly set for me, for you are my tower of strength.
Into your hands I commend my spirit,
For you have redeemed me, O Lord, O God of truth.
I hate those who cling to worthless idols,
And I put my trust in the Lord.
I will rejoice and be glad because of your mercy;
For you have seen my affliction; you know my distress.
You have not shut me up in the power of the enemy;
You have set my feet in an open place.

SIXTH SUNDAY OF EASTER

Acts 17:22-31   Psalm 66:8-20
1 Peter 3:13-22   John 14:15-21

CALL TO WORSHIP

Come and see all that God has done, tremendous in dealing with humanity. Come, listen, all who revere God, and I will tell you all God has done.

PRAYER OF CONFESSION

Giver of commandments, we have received them but have not kept them wholly. Perfect Keeper of commandments, we have not loved fully as you love. Interpreter of commandments, we have resisted the truth, not wanting to know fully what you expect of us. Forgive incomplete obedience, half-hearted love, and evasion of the whole truth. We seek your mercy, your advocacy, and your counsel; through Jesus Christ our Lord. Amen.

DECLARATION OF GOD'S FORGIVENESS

Hear the Good News! Christ died for our sins once and for all. He, the just, suffered for the unjust, to bring us to God. Friends, believe the Good News. *In Jesus Christ, we are forgiven.*

EXHORTATION

Hold the Lord Christ in reverence in your hearts. Always be ready with your defense whenever you are called to account for the hope that is in you, but make that defense with modesty and respect.

PRAYER OF THE DAY

Spirit of truth, grant us such further disclosures of the Father and the Son that we may be aware that God is with us and in us, so that we may lovingly worship you and obey your commandments, even among those who do not receive you; through Jesus Christ, also our advocate with the Father. Amen.

PRAYER OF THANKSGIVING

God everywhere, God with us, God in us, we may find you and know you anywhere. We are grateful that you give us life and breath, together with all human beings. We acknowledge your greatness in designing the world and creating boundaries of time and place. You display great patience with us in our times of ignorance, and delay the day of judgment that we may rediscover you and our solidarity with all humanity. Most of all, you have given us Jesus Christ, raised from the dead, to lead us to repentance and the full knowledge of who we are as offspring of the Eternal. We worship you, O God, Creator, Judge, and Savior. Amen.

PRAYER OF DEDICATION

Ruler of nations and peoples, Head of the church, Spirit of the church, we have vowed to give ourselves in every way as members of the body of Christ. We are here to fulfill our vows and to give substance to our promises. Receive us and our offerings for the strengthening of the church; through Jesus Christ our Lord. Amen.

PSALM 66:8-20

Bless our God, O peoples,
Let the sound of his praise be heard,
Who holds our souls in life,
And will not allow our feet to slip.
For you, O God, have proved us;
You have tried us just as silver is tried.
You brought us into the snare;
You laid heavy burdens upon our backs.
You let enemies ride over our heads; we went
    through fire and water;
But you brought us out into a place of refreshment.
I will enter your house with burnt-offerings
    and will pay you my vows,
Which I promised with my lips and spoke with my mouth
    when I was in trouble.
I will offer you sacrifices of fat beasts with the smoke of rams;
I will give you oxen and goats.
Come and listen, all you who fear God,
And I will tell you what he has done for me.
I called out to him with my mouth,
And his praise was on my tongue.
If I had found evil in my heart,
    the Lord would not have heard me;
The Lord would not have heard me;
    he has attended to the voice of my prayer.
Blessed be God, who has not rejected my prayer,
Nor withheld his love from me.

ASCENSION DAY

Acts 1:1-11   Psalm 47
Ephesians 1:15-23   Luke 24:46-53

CALL TO WORSHIP
Let us worship God.
Let us pray

>   that our inward eyes may be illumined
>   that we may know what is the hope to which God calls us
>   that we may learn how vast are the resources
>   of the Spirit's power
>   that we may value the wealth of the heritage
>   that we share with Christ.

PRAYER OF CONFESSION
*God of Moses, God of the Messiah, God of the church, forgive the
doubts that plague us, the questions as to your timetable for
history, the fears that the events of our time are beyond all
control, even yours. Excuse our slowness in fulfilling our mission
of proclaiming to all nations the name of Jesus and the repentance
which brings forgiveness of sins. We need such forgiveness
ourselves, for we have not properly acknowledged your majesty
and power, nor received your gracious enablement to complete
your work in the world. Have patience with us and the whole
body of the church of which Jesus Christ is the head, in his name.
Amen.*

DECLARATION OF GOD'S FORGIVENESS
Hear the Good News! Jesus sent his Father's promised gift of the
Holy Spirit to arm us with power from above. Friends, believe the
Good News. *In Jesus Christ, we are forgiven.*

EXHORTATION
Keep your minds open to understand the Scriptures, for all that
was written in the Law of Moses and in the prophets and in the
psalms were bound to be fulfilled in Jesus Christ. Be prepared to
be a witness to all these things.

PRAYER OF THE DAY
*God of our Lord Jesus Christ, all-glorious Parent, bless us with
such insightful faith that we may worship you with great joy,
spending in your house enough time to prepare us to be your*

witnesses everywhere in the world, by the power of the Holy Spirit. Amen.

PRAYER OF THANKSGIVING

We praise you, Lord Christ, ascended to the right hand of divine sovereignty. Since your mother, Mary, bore you, you have been resplendent in holiness. The symbol of your power is the empty cross, for you have vanquished sin and death. In the Spirit, you give your church powers of wisdom and vision. Thanks to you, Son of God, we are given knowledge of the Father, and thanks to you, Divine Spirit, we are given knowledge of the Son and the inspiration to witness before the world the Good News entrusted to the Church. Amen.

PRAYER OF DEDICATION

Our resources are limited, Lord God, but yours are not. What we give is multiplied beyond measure when we open ourselves to being used by the Spirit enlivening the church of the Beloved Son. Amen.

PSALM 47

Clap your hands, all you peoples;
Shout to God with a cry of joy.
For the Lord Most High is to be feared;
He is the great King over all the earth.
He subdues the peoples under us,
And the nations under our feet.
He chooses our inheritance for us,
The pride of Jacob whom he loves.
God has gone up with a shout,
The Lord with the sound of the ram's horn.
Sing praises to God, sing praises;
Sing praises to our King, sing praises.
For God is king of all the earth;
Sing praises with all your skill.
God reigns over the nations;
God sits upon his holy throne.
The nobles of the peoples have gathered together
    with the people of the God of Abraham.
The rulers of the earth belong to God, and he is highly exalted.

SEVENTH SUNDAY OF EASTER

Acts 1:6-14   Psalm 68:1-10
1 Peter 4:12-14; 5:6-11   John 17:1-11

CALL TO WORSHIP

Worship God, the sovereign Lawgiver of Sinai. Worship the One who ascends from the hill called Olive. Receive the Spirit without whom we cannot truly worship.

PRAYER OF CONFESSION

God of all grace, Christ of glory, powerful Spirit, we confess that the tempter sometimes catches us unawares. When things are going well for us, pride in our deserving such prosperity may be the very cause of our downfall. When we are convinced that we can get by on our own, unexpected reverses can drag us down with anxiety. Then we are tempted to believe that you do not care and cannot bring us through our time of adversity. Restore, establish, and strengthen us in the faith of Jesus Christ. Amen.

DECLARATION OF GOD'S FORGIVENESS

Hear the Good News! The Spirit of God is resting upon us and will give us cause for joy as we are willing to share the suffering of Christ. Friends, believe the Good News. *In Jesus Christ, we are forgiven.*

EXHORTATION

Humble yourselves under the almighty hand of God, who will lift you up in due time and cares for you always.

PRAYER OF THE DAY

Holy Parent, protect us as our Savior has prayed, that we may not seek independence, but unity, the unity of love and obedience, so that the world also may believe in the One you have sent, Jesus your Son. Amen.

PRAYER OF THANKSGIVING

Great Sovereign over all the earth, you are high above the most powerful of earth's royalty and mighty ones. We are grateful for our heritage of faith from the days of Abraham, to the apostles, to the present day. We are privileged to pray in the company of all the faithful in this and every generation. Though we are undeserving, we are honored to bear the name of Christ, having heard and heeded the Good News of Jesus Christ. Receive our

74

thanksgiving for all the prayers of Christ and others for us and for the unity of your church, to the glory of your name. Amen.

PRAYER OF DEDICATION
At prayer together before you, God of the Gospel, we come as adults and children to obey the Gospel and do the good to which you point us, moved by the Spirit to share the work and the suffering of Jesus Christ. Amen.

PSALM 68:1-10
Let God arise, and let his enemies be scattered;
Let those who hate him flee before him.
Let them vanish like smoke when the wind drives it away;
As the wax melts at the fire,
    so let the wicked perish at the presence of God.
But let the righteous be glad and rejoice before God;
Let them also be merry and joyful.
Sing to God, sing praises to his Name;
Exhalt him who rides upon the heavens;
Yahweh is his Name, rejoice before him!
Father of orphans, defender of widows,
    God in his holy habitation!
God gives the solitary a home
    and brings forth prisoners into freedom;
But the rebels shall live in dry places.
O God, when you went forth before your people,
When you marched through the wilderness,
The earth shook, and the skies poured down rain
    at the presence of God, the God of Sinai.
At the presence of God, the God of Israel.
You sent a gracious rain, O God, upon your inheritance;
You refreshed the land when it was weary.
Your people found their home in it;
In your goodness, O God, you have made provision for the poor.

PENTECOST

Acts 2:1-21 (or Isaiah 44:1-8)   Psalm 104:24-33
1 Corinthians 12:3b-13 (or Acts 2:1-21)   John 20:19-23 (or 7:37-39)

CALL TO WORSHIP
Let us sing to our Creator as long as we live. May our meditations please our God to whom we show our joy.

PRAYER OF CONFESSION
Creator God, personal God, Giver of life, your works of nature are countless, your patience with humankind seems endless, your gifts of grace are various. We do not appreciate the wisdom of your creating genius without continued study and wonder. We take for granted too many of the creatures to which you have given life in our earth and sea and sky. We forget to give thanks and to bring praise to your name. We are jealous of the gifts you have given others and fail to use the particular gifts you have given us. Forgive the neglect of our gifts and of the opportunities to use them in the body of Christ, the church; through Jesus Christ our Lord. Amen.

DECLARATION OF GOD'S FORGIVENESS
Hear the Good News! We were all brought into one body by baptism, in the one Spirit, whatever our language and nationality, whatever our place in society, and that One Spirit was poured out for all of us to drink. Friends, believe the Good News. *In Jesus Christ, we are forgiven.*

EXHORTATION
There are a variety of gifts, but the same Spirit. There are varieties of service, but the same Lord. There are many forms of work, but all of them, in all, are the work of the same God. Use your gifts for some useful purpose.

PRAYER OF THE DAY
Holy Spirit, given One, gift of God, the Sender and the Sent, grant us continuing peace and the gift of discernment, that we may be as forgiving as you are, and as true in expecting repentance in others as in ourselves. Amen.

PRAYER OF THANKSGIVING
God of variety, we give thanks for your many and varied gifts to the church; for gifts of wise speech, putting deep knowledge into

words; for gifts of faith and healing of mind and body; for the gifts
of prophecy and discernment of truth and falsehood; for ecstatic
speech and music and the ability to interpret it. We rejoice in the
unity that is possible when these gifts are received willingly and
coordinated by the Spirit as the activity of the one Body of Christ.
We celebrate that unity of one Lord, one faith, one baptism, one
work. May your glory stand forever, that you may rejoice in your
own work in nature and in the church. Amen.

PRAYER OF DEDICATION
God all glorious, there is nothing we can tell you that you do not
know. There is nothing we can give you that you have not made
possible. Though you have given us the freedom to be silent and
to withhold our gifts, we offer our prayers and our gifts; in the
name and spirit of Jesus Christ. Amen.

PSALM 104:24-33
Man goes forth to his work
And to his labor until the evening.
O Lord, how manifold are your works!
In wisdom you have made them all;
    the earth is full of your creatures.
Yonder is the great and wide sea with its living things
    too many to number, creatures both small and great.
There move the ships, and there is that Leviathan,
    which you have made for the sport of it.
All of them look to you to give them their food in due season.
You give it to them; they gather it;
You open your hand, and they are filled with good things.
You hide your face, and they are terrified;
You take away their breath, and they die and return to their dust.
You send forth your Spirit, and they are created;
    and so you renew the face of the earth.
May the glory of the Lord endure for ever;
May the Lord rejoice in all his works.
He looks at the earth and it trembles;
He touches the mountains and they smoke.
I will sing to the Lord as long as I live;
I will praise my God while I have my being.

FIRST SUNDAY AFTER PENTECOST (TRINITY)

Deuteronomy 4:32-40   Psalm 33
2 Corinthians 13:5-14   Matthew 28:16-20

CALL TO WORSHIP

Ascribe to the Lord the glory due to his name; bow down to the Lord in the splendor of holiness.

PRAYER OF CONFESSION

God of love, Son of grace, Spirit of community, it is easier for us to recite the creed than to test our living by the faith. Self-examination can be painful and we would rather not be put to the test. When we have seen that we are off the track, we do not readily mend our ways. We may exchange the kiss of peace around your table, but we are not always as agreeable in committee meetings. We want to live in peace, but sometimes do so only by withdrawing from people with whom we disagree. Grant us your loving forgiveness, that we may be gracious to those with whom we differ and not break up the community you mean to be unified in the Spirit, for Jesus' sake. Amen.

DECLARATION OF GOD'S FORGIVENESS

Hear the Good News! The Lord will give strength to his people. The Lord will bless his people with peace. Friends, believe the Good News. *In Jesus Christ, we are forgiven.*

EXHORTATION

Mend your ways; agree with one another; live in peace; and the God of peace will be with you.

PRAYER OF THE DAY

Sovereign Lord of heaven and earth, reassure all doubtful disciples of your authority, that they may be obedient to their commission to call all nations to discipleship, baptizing in the name of the Father, the Son and the Holy Spirit. Amen.

PRAYER OF THANKSGIVING

We rejoice in the knowledge of you, O God, for you love righteousness and justice and your love unfailing fills the earth. Your plans will survive when the plans of nations come to nothing. We give thanks to you with all the musical arts we have mastered. They are but faint praise beside the music of the stars and the majesty of the seas. We stand in awe of the power of creation you have exercised in the scattering of the stars and the gathering of the seas. We are humbly grateful that you receive us as your people for the sake of Jesus Christ. Amen.

PRAYER OF DEDICATION

Without the wisdom and fullness of the Spirit, your church, O God, cannot spread the word and increase the number of disciples. Bless both those who give themselves to prayer and the ministry of the word, and those who are responsible for the distribution of the gifts we bring, through Jesus Christ our Lord. Amen.

PSALM 33:1-11

Rejoice in the Lord, you righteous;
It is good for the just to sing praises.
Praise the Lord with the harp;
Play to him upon the psaltery and lyre.
Sing for him a new song;
Sound a fanfare with all your skill upon the trumpet.
For the word of the Lord is right,
And all his works are sure.
He loves righteousness and justice;
The loving-kindness of the Lord fills the whole earth.
By the word of the Lord were the heavens made,
By the breath of his mouth all the heavenly hosts.
He gathers up the waters of the ocean as in a water-skin
And stores up the depths of the sea.
Let all the earth fear the Lord;
Let all who dwell in the world stand in awe of him.
For he spoke, and it came to pass;
He commanded, and it stood fast.
The Lord brings the will of the nations to naught;
He thwarts the designs of the peoples.
But the Lord's will stands fast forever,
And the designs of his heart from age to age.

SECOND SUNDAY AFTER PENTECOST

Genesis 12:1-9   Psalm 33:12-22
Romans 3:21-28   Matthew 7:21-29

CALL TO WORSHIP
In this place of prayer let us invoke God by name, that we may
know God's gracious blessing.

PRAYER OF CONFESSION
*Truthful God, liberating Christ, humbling Spirit, we confess that
we have sinned and are deprived of the divine splendor. We are not
nearly as good as we were meant to be. Both the law and the
prophets have clarified your justice and your willingness to justify
us as we accept the sacrificial death of Christ for our sins. We
have no reason for self-righteous pride, but should be humble in
gratitude for your free grace. Overlook the sins of our past and any
unjustified pride, for the sake of the liberating Christ, who is
making us free. Amen.*

DECLARATION OF GOD'S FORGIVENESS
Hear the Good News! All are justified by God's free grace alone,
through his act of liberation in the person of Christ Jesus. For
God designed him to be the means of expiating sin by his
sacrificial death, effective through faith. Friends, believe the
Good News. *In Jesus Christ, we are forgiven.*

EXHORTATION
Do not brag about keeping the commandments. Justification by
faith excludes such pride.

PRAYER OF THE DAY
*Lord Jesus Christ, let us not call you Lord in vain, but both hear
and act on the words you speak, that our lives may be firmly
founded on the rock of God's will, and indestructible in the midst
of the storms of life. Amen.*

PRAYER OF THANKSGIVING
*Heavenly Parent, God of our ancestors, we thank you for all our
fathers and mothers in the faith, natural parents and adopting
parents, foster parents, and others who have been significant in
the shaping of our minds and feelings, our ideas and our values,
our goals and our behavior. We are grateful for the learning
experiences that have strengthened our faith, memories that draw*

us to your house and to other places hallowed by awareness of your presence, occasions of sympathy and understanding too intimate to explain. We celebrate every home marked with signs of your faithful love, not only with art and symbol, but also with hospitality and human caring. Your truth is our foundation rock; your unfailing love, our shelter; your will, the walls that guard our way of life. All praise to you, God of all lands, all people, our people. Amen.

PRAYER OF DEDICATION

We can only present what you freely give, gracious God. We express our faith and our thanksgiving in these offerings, that the church may continue to witness your justice, through the law, the prophets and the gospel of your liberating Son, Jesus Christ. Amen.

PSALM 33:12-22

Happy is the nation whose God is the Lord!
Happy the people he has chosen to be his own!
The Lord looks down from heaven,
 and beholds all the people in the world.
From where he sits enthroned he turns his gaze
 on all who dwell on the earth.
He fashions all the hearts of them
And understands all their works.
There is no king that can be saved by a mighty army;
A strong man is not delivered by his great strength.
The horse is a vain hope for deliverance;
For all its strength it cannot save.
Behold, the eye of the Lord is upon those who fear him,
On those who wait upon his love,
To pluck their lives from death,
And to feed them in time of famine.
Our soul waits for the Lord;
He is our help and our shield.
Indeed, our heart rejoices in him,
For in his holy Name we put our trust.
Let your loving-kindness, O Lord, be upon us,
As we have put our trust in you.

THIRD SUNDAY AFTER PENTECOST

Genesis 22:1-18   Psalm 13
Romans 4:13-18   Matthew 9:9-13

CALL TO WORSHIP
Let us trust in God's true love, rejoicing that we have been set free.

PRAYER OF CONFESSION
God of life, God of healing, God of health, though we are reluctant to say that there is no health in us, we do confess that we are not in perfect spiritual health. We are grateful that Jesus came to call bad characters, as a doctor is sent to heal the sick. Save us from the pride which prevents our taking all the prescriptions of this healer of the soul, Jesus of Nazareth. Teach us also what it means to be merciful, that we may not shun the company of less discreet sinners in the church. Be our healer until we at last attain spiritual wholeness. Amen.

DECLARATION OF GOD'S FORGIVENESS
Hear the Good News! Jesus said, I did not come to invite virtuous people, but sinners. Friends, believe the Good News. *In Jesus Christ, we are forgiven.*

EXHORTATION
As he said to Matthew, so Jesus says to you: "Follow me."

PRAYER OF THE DAY
Good Teacher, send us among those who need to hear your invitation to discipleship, that we may share the Good News and express your mercy toward all sinners. Amen.

PRAYER OF THANKSGIVING
God of Abraham and Sarah, we rejoice in your promises. Through them, father and mother of many nations, we have come to inherit the gift of faith in you, who makes the dead live and summons things that are not yet in existence as if they already were. We thank you for Jesus our Lord whom you raised from the dead, for he was given up to death for our misdeeds and raised to life to justify us. Your promises to us are a matter of sheer grace which we receive by faith and not by upholding the law. We honor you, God, for freely justifying us. We call you Lord, Jesus Christ, for your death and resurrection. We receive you, divine Spirit, as an

82

undeserved gift of eternal life. Amen.

PRAYER OF DEDICATION

Gracious God, the death of Christ on the cross precludes any offering for our sins. Receive what we give and our promised service as a response in thanksgiving, through Jesus Christ, Lamb of God, Savior of the world. Amen.

PSALM 13

How long, O Lord? Will you forget me for ever?
How long will you hide your face from me?
How long shall I have perplexity in my mind,
    and grief in my heart, day after day?
How long shall my enemy triumph over me?
Look upon me and answer me, O Lord my God;
Give light to my eyes, lest I sleep in death;
Lest my enemy say, "I have prevailed over him"
And my foes rejoice that I have fallen.
But I put my trust in your mercy:
My heart is joyful because of your saving help.
I will sing to the Lord, for he has dealt with me richly;
I will praise the Name of the Lord Most High.

FOURTH SUNDAY AFTER PENTECOST

Genesis 25:19-34
Romans 5:6-11

Psalm 46
Matthew 9:35-10:8

CALL TO WORSHIP

Let us exult in God through our Lord Jesus Christ, through whom we have been granted reconciliation, proving God's love for us sinners.

PRAYER OF CONFESSION

Creator of the way, Finder of the lost, Guide of the trusting, we confess that we are helpless to save ourselves, that we have been willful and have left the way even when we have seen it clearly, that we have harassed others as they have harassed us, that self-control might have spared us some of our illnesses and that our weaknesses can be overcome only by the health and strength you can give in spirit and soul and body. Forgive our sins. Heal our diseases. Have pity on us as did Jesus of Nazareth. Amen.

DECLARATION OF GOD'S FORGIVENESS

Hear the Good News! God has shown us how much he loves us. It was while we were yet sinners that Christ died for us. Friends, believe the Good News. *In Jesus Christ, we are forgiven.*

EXHORTATION

Rejoice in God through our Lord Jesus Christ, who has now made us God's friends.

PRAYER OF THE DAY

Patient Leader, help us to know our best skills, that we may find the place of greatest usefulness to people in need and so extend your ministry of love and healing and spread the Good News of the kingdom. Name us and number us also among your disciples. Amen.

PRAYER OF THANKSGIVING

Loving God, dying Son, living Lord, how amazingly you prove your love for us! Though you might have cast us off forever in anger at our sins, you show your loving forgiveness in the death of your Son and our Lord, Jesus Christ. We rejoice in the sacrificial death that saves us and the ongoing life that intercedes for us. We are filled with joyful trust and thanksgiving that you have befriended us. Weak and unworthy as we are, we thank you for your love. You are worthy of all praise, critical but conciliatory God, human and divine Christ, holy and hopeful Spirit. Amen.

PRAYER OF DEDICATION

Gracious God, your love is everlasting and your constancy endures to all generations. Our gifts are limited and our voices will fade, but we want our children and our grandchildren and our nephews and our nieces to worship you in gladness in this place; through Jesus Christ our Savior. Amen.

PSALM 46

God is our refuge and strength,
A very present help in trouble.
Therefore we will not fear, though the earth be moved,
And though the mountains be toppled into the depths of the sea;
Though its waters rage and foam,
And though the mountains tremble at its tumult.
The Lord of hosts is with us;
The God of Jacob is our stronghold.
There is a river whose streams make glad the city of God,
The holy habitation of the Most High.
God is in the midst of her; she shall not be overthrown;
God shall help her at the break of day.
The nations make much ado, and the kingdoms are shaken;
God has spoken, and the earth shall melt away.
The Lord of hosts is with us;
The God of Jacob is our stronghold.
Come now and look upon the works of the Lord,
What awesome things he has done on earth.
It is he who makes war to cease in all the world;
He breaks the bow, and shatters the spear,
    and burns the shields with fire.
"Be still, then, and know that I am God;
I will be exalted among the nations; I will be exalted in the earth."
The Lord of hosts is with us;
The God of Jacob is our stronghold.

FIFTH SUNDAY AFTER PENTECOST

Genesis 28:10-17   Psalm 91:1-10
Romans 5:12-19   Matthew 10:24-33

CALL TO WORSHIP
Lodge under the shadow of the Almighty; live in the shelter of
the Most High; our God is a safe retreat; we make the Most High
our refuge.

PRAYER OF CONFESSION
*Meticulous God of immeasurable grace, how shall we measure
our sins? Only you know their real dimensions; the history of
human disobedience; the ramifications of hatred, greed, and lust;
the multiplication of wrongdoing by generations; the perpetuation
of prejudices by unthinking repetition; the aggravation of offenses
by the unforgiving and vengeful. However you account for our
sin, there are none of us who do not stand in need of some
measure of your grace, which in Jesus Christ is out of all
proportion to human wrongdoing. Amen.*

DECLARATION OF GOD'S FORGIVENESS
Hear the Good News! God's act of grace is out of all proportion
to human wrongdoing, the gift that came to so many by the grace
of the one man, Jesus Christ. Friends, believe the Good News. *In
Jesus Christ, we are forgiven.*

EXHORTATION
Do not fear those who kill the body, but cannot kill the soul. Fear
him rather who is able to destroy both soul and body in hell.

PRAYER OF THE DAY
*Creator of all life, reassuring Parent, help us to tell simply and
clearly the promises of your love and care that we have received
in secret so that our brothers and sisters who live in doubt and fear
may trust you as well; through Jesus Christ our Lord. Amen.*

PRAYER OF THANKSGIVING
*We give thanks to you, O God, that the gate of heaven may be
found in any place, and your house wherever we receive your
revelation. You send your messengers to us in both waking and
sleeping hours, to comfort and reassure us of your constant care
and love. You reaffirm to us promises old and new, in law and
gospel, in word and sacrament. Receive our praise, Guardian of*

sparrows and of sinners, Teacher of the simple, Enlightener of all who seek light in darkness. Amen.

PRAYER OF DEDICATION

Though we are bound to serve you, divine Superior, we do not serve you without fault. Achieve your purposes through the church, despite our imperfect commitment to service, and the reproach of the world, to the glory of your name. Amen.

PSALM 91:1-10

He who dwells in the shelter of the Most High,
Abides under the shadow of the Almighty.
He shall say to the Lord, "You are my refuge and my stronghold,
My God in whom I put my trust."
He shall deliver you from the snare of the hunter
    and from the deadly pestilence.
He shall cover you with his pinions,
And you shall find refuge under his wings;
His faithfulness shall be a shield and buckler.
You shall not be afraid of any terror by night,
Nor of the arrow that flies by day;
Of the plague that stalks in the darkness,
Nor of the sickness that lays waste at mid-day.
A thousand shall fall at your side
And ten thousand at your right hand,
But it shall not come near you.
Your eyes have only to behold to see the reward of the wicked
Because you have made the Lord your refuge,
And the Most High your habitation,
There shall no evil happen to you,
Neither shall any plague come near your dwelling.

SIXTH SUNDAY AFTER PENTECOST

Genesis 32:22-32
Romans 6:3-11

Psalm 17:1-7, 15
Matthew 10:34-42

CALL TO WORSHIP

Let us call upon God to answer us. Let us not be satisfied until we see God's likeness.

PRAYER OF CONFESSION

Perfect Parent, worthy Son, uniting Spirit, our love for you is not as worthy of you as it should be. Other loves compete in us for our response. Our feet have been set upon a new path of life through our baptism into Christ. We admit that we stray from that way, returning to the ways of death that should be left behind. We presume upon your grace by our sinning rather than draw upon the new life that is available to us in union with Christ Jesus. Forgive us for allowing your life and love to go so unrequited, for the sake of your devoted Son, Jesus Christ. Amen.

DECLARATION OF GOD'S FORGIVENESS

Hear the Good News! Remember that in baptism we were baptized into the death and resurrection of Jesus Christ, so that we may no longer be the slaves of sin, but alive to God. Friends, believe the Good News. *In Jesus Christ, we are forgiven.*

EXHORTATION

Set your feet upon the new path of life in the company of Jesus and leave behind the old ways of sin and death.

PRAYER OF THE DAY

Divine-Human, Cross-Bearer and Leader, lead us away from goals that have been set by our families or ourselves, goals that are short of your purposes for us and for your whole family, that we may be worthy disciples and cross-bearers, for your sake. Amen.

PRAYER OF THANKSGIVING

Maker of covenants, we are grateful for your generous spirit in condescending to be partners with us in human governments and enterprises. Death-accepting, to-life-returning Christ, we are thankful for the baptism you share with us that we may know the splendor that lies beyond the dominion of sin and death. Giver of rewards, we are undeserving of the attention you give to the simplest acts of humanity and generosity. We are thankful for all

88

the promises you have made and kept. We live in hope of the completion of the new creation you have undertaken as the kingdom of Jesus Christ. Amen.

PRAYER OF DEDICATION
Divine Overseer, if even a cup of water for one of your disciples does not go unnoticed, then our offerings to support your ministers and the work of your church will also be rewarded. Grant us also the share of the prophet's reward and the blessing that comes in the company of good people. Amen.

PSALM 17:1-7, 15
Hear my plea of innocence, O Lord; give heed to my cry;
Listen to my prayer, which does not come from lying lips.
Let my vindication come forth from your presence;
Let your eyes be fixed on justice.
Weigh my heart, summon me by night,
Melt me down; you will find no impurity in me.
I give no offense with my mouth as others do;
I have heeded the words of your lips.
My footsteps hold fast to the ways of your law;
In your paths my feet shall not stumble.
I call upon you, O God, for you will answer me;
Incline your ear to me and hear my words.
Show me your marvelous loving-kindness,
O Savior of those who take refuge at your right hand
     from those who rise up against them.
But at my vindication I shall see your face;
When I awake, I shall be satisfied, beholding your likeness.

SEVENTH SUNDAY AFTER PENTECOST

Exodus 1:6-14,1:22-2:10   Psalm 124
Romans 7:14-25a   Matthew 11:25-30

CALL TO WORSHIP
Hear the invitation of Jesus: "Come to me, all those whose work
is hard, whose load is heavy; and I will give you relief. Bend your
necks to my yoke, and learn from me, for I am gentle and
humble-hearted; and your souls will find relief. For my yoke is
good to bear, my load is light."

PRAYER OF CONFESSION
*Liberator of slaves, Deliverer of the endangered, Teacher of the
simple, both nations and individuals look to you for
emancipation. Our sins oppress us, the sins within us and the
sinners around us. Our racial and national pride too often drive us
to ruthlessness in the treatment of others. Unbridled ambition is
served at the expense of others. When sin tyrannizes us, we
tyrannize others. Forgive our self-serving sins and free us to serve
in the yoke of Christ, the One for others. Amen.*

DECLARATION OF GOD'S FORGIVENESS
Hear the Good News! God alone frees us from the rule of sin in
our own natures, through Jesus Christ. Friends, believe the Good
News! *In Jesus Christ, we are forgiven.*

EXHORTATION
Learn from Jesus, who is gentle and humble-hearted and you will
find that working with him is comfortable and not too difficult.

PRAYER OF THE DAY
*Ruler of heaven and earth, disclose to us in our simplicity all we
need to know of your judgment, that we may not carry loads of
guilt too much for us to bear, but, experiencing your forgiveness
and relief, may serve easily in the light yoke with Jesus Christ.
Amen.*

PRAYER OF THANKSGIVING
*You are our Creator and Helper, O God. When illness or accident
have endangered our lives, we have been spared and life seems
more precious to us. When our lives have been extended and we
sense their value, we have committed ourselves to your service
with new sincerity and energy. We are grateful that we do not*

serve you alone, but may enjoy the company and support of others and especially the nearness of your yokefellow, Jesus Christ. Amen.

PRAYER OF DEDICATION

Master Worker, we bend our necks to your yoke and will learn to serve with you as you teach us. Use us and all that is ours to accomplish with humility and good humor the high purposes of your church, to the glory of your name. Amen.

PSALM 124

If the Lord had not been on our side, let Israel now say;
If the Lord had not been on our side,
    when enemies rose up against us;
Then would they have swallowed us up alive
    in their fierce anger toward us;
Then would the waters have overwhelmed us
    and the torrent gone over us;
Then would the raging waters have gone right over us.
Blessed be the Lord! He has not given us over
    to be a prey for their teeth.
We have escaped like a bird from the snare of the fowler;
The snare is broken, and we have escaped.
OUR HELP IS IN THE NAME OF THE LORD,
    THE MAKER OF HEAVEN AND EARTH.

EIGHTH SUNDAY AFTER PENTECOST

Exodus 2:11-22   Psalm 69:6-15
Romans 8:9-17   Matthew 13:1-9, 18-23

CALL TO WORSHIP

The Spirit who adopts us as children of God enables us to pray
with confidence to our divine Parent, with all the ease and
familiarity of small children to earthly parents. Pray then as a
little child.

PRAYER OF CONFESSION

*Persistent Word-Creator, patient Teacher, persuasive Spirit, you
are tireless in speaking to us, but we find it easy to close our
minds, to refuse to hear what would require growth and painful
change, to reject the truth because it is inconvenient. Forgive
deliberate denseness of mind, fearful resistance to change,
stubborn insistence that our way is the best way. Continue your
speaking until we hear. Try new parables on us until we think and
understand. Argue with us until we do your will. What else will
your love in Christ allow you to do? Amen.*

DECLARATION OF GOD'S FORGIVENESS

Hear the Good News! All who are moved by the Spirit of God are
children of God and heirs of God's splendor with Jesus Christ.
Friends, believe the Good News! *In Jesus Christ, we are forgiven.*

EXHORTATION

Do not be content simply to do what comes naturally. Live on
the spiritual level as a Christian in whom Christ dwells by the
Spirit.

PRAYER OF THE DAY

*God of mystery, Sharer of divine secrets, Spirit of God's whole
family, enable us to hear what you speak, to see what you
disclose, to respond as to a parent in our prayers, that we may be
strengthened to share the suffering of Christ, our Brother, and live
free from fear until the day of splendor comes. Amen.*

PRAYER OF THANKSGIVING

*Creator of the visible and the invisible, divine Deliverer, life-
sustaining Spirit, all that is depends upon you and rejoices in your
praise. You blot out our sins and free us to live as your children in
love and helpfulness. Your spirit both inspires our prayers and*

promotes our growth in grace and in the likeness of Jesus Christ. All whom you deliver from sin and death praise you in your household. We especially rejoice in the reassuring voice of the Spirit, calling us into one loving family with you, Father, Son and Mothering Spirit. Amen.

PRAYER OF DEDICATION

Holy Parent, you relieve us from the burden of our guilt and save us from the loneliness that isolates us from others and from you. With these, our offerings, we pledge our vows of service in the company of this holy family, in the Spirit of Jesus Christ. Amen.

PSALM 69:6-15

O God, you know my foolishness,
And my faults are not hidden from you.
Let not those who hope in you be put to shame through me, Lord God of hosts;
Let not those who seek you be disgraced because of me, O God of Israel.
Surely, for your sake have I suffered reproach,
And shame has covered my face.
I have become a stranger to my own kindred,
An alien to my mother's children.
Zeal for your house has eaten me up;
The scorn of those who scorn you has fallen upon me.
I humbled myself with fasting, but that was turned to my reproach.
I put on sack-cloth also, and became a byword among them.
Those who sit at the gate murmur against me,
And the drunkards make songs about me.
But as for me, this is my prayer to you, at the time you have set, O Lord;
"In your great mercy, O God, answer me with your unfailing help.
Save me from the mire; do not let me sink;
Let me be rescued from those who hate me and out of the deep waters.
Let not the torrent of waters wash over me, neither let the deep swallow me up;
Do not let the Pit shut its mouth upon me."

NINTH SUNDAY AFTER PENTECOST

Exodus 3:1-12　　　　　　　　　　　　　　　　Psalm 103:1-13
Romans 8:18-25　　　　　　　　　　　　Matthew 13:24-30, 36-43

CALL TO WORSHIP
Let us bless God from our innermost hearts, forgetting none of
the benefits of God's compassion: pardon for our guilt, healing
for our suffering, constant love and renewal of strength.

PRAYER OF CONFESSION
*God of long-range planning, God involved in human history, God
who saves us in hope, we confess that we are impatient with your
timing. We want immediate judgment on the sins of others,
though not on our own. The time of our own suffering seems
endless, but the duration of deprivation for others we can shrug
off. We want instant recognition of our achievements, but are
jealous of the honors afforded others. Forgive the pride that
proposes, that we know better than you do, what should be done
and when, for the sake of Jesus of Nazareth, who also struggled
against doing your will but did it nevertheless. Amen.*

DECLARATION OF GOD'S FORGIVENESS
Hear the Good News! We have been saved, though only in hope
of the splendor which is in store for us. Friends, believe the Good
News. *In Jesus Christ, we are forgiven.*

EXHORTATION
Endure suffering and frustration in hope of entering into the
liberty and splendor of the children of God.

PRAYER OF THE DAY
*Nourish our hopes with prophetic promises, eternal God, and
keep us awake in searching out your secrets, that our timeline may
be sychronized with yours, as was the earthly time of your Son,
Jesus Christ. Amen.*

PRAYER OF THANKSGIVING
*Obscure God, disclosed through a strange history and a suffering
Son of an insignificant nation, we stand in awe of your mysterious
ways. Who is there to be compared with you? You only are God.
We have never heard of anyone who can do what you do. You
bring to power the powerless and overthrow the tyrant. You are
compassionate and gracious, showing your favor to slaves as well*

as sovereigns, promising liberty to all who live in hope of the final triumph of your goodness. In a blighted world, we rejoice in the first fruits that point to a final harvest still to come. In mortality, we wait with eager anticipation for the freedom of immortality. We praise you, God of creation, God of resurrection, God of restoration. Amen.

PRAYER OF DEDICATION

Multiplier of small things, make of us a force for good, uplifting what is best in our community, to the glory of your name and the growth of your rule in the world. Amen.

PSALM 103:1-13

Bless the Lord, O my soul,
And all that is within me, bless his holy Name.
Bless the Lord, O my soul,
And forget not all his benefits.
He forgives all your sins
And heals all your infirmities;
He redeems your life from the grave
And crowns you with mercy and loving-kindness;
He satisfies you with good things,
And your youth is renewed like an eagle's.
The Lord executes righteousness and judgment for all who are oppressed.
He made his ways known to Moses and his works to the children of Israel.
The Lord is full of compassion and mercy, slow to anger and of great kindness.
He will not always accuse us, nor will he keep his anger forever.
He has not dealt with us according to our sins,
Nor rewarded us according to our wickedness.
For as the heavens are high above the earth, so is his mercy great upon those who fear him.
As far as the east is from the west, so far has he removed our sins from us.
As a father cares for his children,
So does the Lord care for those who fear him.

TENTH SUNDAY AFTER PENTECOST

Exodus 3:13-20   Psalm 105:1-11
Romans 8:26-30   Matthew 13:44-52

CALL TO WORSHIP
Give God thanks and invoke the hallowed name, making God's
deeds known the world around. Do this honor with song and
psalm and think upon all of the wonders of God.

PRAYER OF CONFESSION
*Supreme Communicator, who can explain how you hear and
speak to us? Divine-Human Communication, how shall we
properly acknowledge you as one who teaches and is the
teaching? Internal Communicator, how can you be God and
within us, unworthy and unknowing as we are? Yet we frequently
live without adequate time set aside for prayer and meditation,
smug in our small wisdom, self-satisfied and self-righteous, though
still so unlike your eldest son, our Brother, Jesus. Forgive our
misplaced values, for not treasuring your complete rule in us at
the cost of all else. Our only hope is that you will continue to
shape us in our life as your family with Jesus Christ. Amen.*

DECLARATION OF GOD'S FORGIVENESS
Hear the Good News! God knew his own before they ever were.
He calls us, justifies us, and gives us the splendor of the brothers
and sisters of Jesus Christ. Friends, believe the Good News. *In
Jesus Christ, we are forgiven.*

EXHORTATION
Cling to nothing as having any worth, besides the knowledge of
the dominion of heaven and the privilege of being a learner in it.

PRAYER OF THE DAY
*Teller of parables, we need to learn in order to teach, but teach us
by your tantalizing parables, that our imaginations may be
stretched and we will tell new parables as well as old ones. Amen.*

PRAYER OF THANKSGIVING
*Hearer of prayers, Giver of wisdom, Advocate of God's people, we
give thanks for every human leader who has sought and received
your gifts: who has known and served you by whatever name. We
thank you for patriarchs and matriarchs, that you are the God of
Sarah as well as of Abraham, of Rebecca as well as of Isaac, of*

Rachel as well as of Jacob. You make yourself known in days of pilgrimage as in years of exile and in periods of settlement. There is no place on earth where you cannot be worshiped and called upon, by whatever name or title, in any language, by people of many faults and different customs. You deserve the thanksgiving of everyone everywhere, for you are God of all, responsive, generous, compassionate. Amen.

PRAYER OF DEDICATION

How can we set a price on the parables of the kingdom, or consider an admission charge to enter into your realm, Sovereign of sovereigns? Receive us, undeserving as we are, for the sake of our elder Brother, Jesus, Prince of Peace, and sanctify these humble gifts by the Spirit's use. Amen.

PSALM 105:1-11

Give thanks to the Lord and call upon his Name;
Make known his deeds among the peoples.
Sing to him, sing praises to him,
And speak of all his marvelous works.
Glory in his holy Name;
Let the hearts of those who seek the Lord rejoice.
Search for the Lord and his strength;
Continually seek his face.
Remember the marvels he has done,
His wonders and the judgments of his mouth,
O offspring of Abraham his servant,
O children of Jacob his chosen.
He is the Lord our God;
His judgments prevail in all the world.
He has always been mindful of his covenant,
The promise he made for a thousand generations:
The covenant he made with Abraham,
The oath that he swore to Isaac,
Which he established as a statute for Jacob,
An everlasting covenant for Israel,
Saying, "To you will I give the land of Canaan
To be your allotted inheritance."

ELEVENTH SUNDAY AFTER PENTECOST

Exodus 12:1-14
Romans 8:31-39

Psalm 143:1-10
Matthew 14:13-21

CALL TO WORSHIP
In the morning come to know God's true love and put your trust in the gracious kindness of the eternal One.

PRAYER OF CONFESSION
Unsparing God, pleading Christ, satisfying Spirit, we confess that we spend a lot of time and energy in the pursuit of what does not satisfy for long. We forget your promises and provisions and fall into times of depression and despair. We underestimate the extent of your love and the lavishness of your gifts. Forgive such doubt and ingratitude and bring us to the overwhelming victory that is ours through Jesus Christ who loved us and loves us still. Amen.

DECLARATION OF GOD'S FORGIVENESS
Hear the Good News. Nothing in all creation can separate us from the love of God in Christ Jesus. Friends, believe the Good News. *In Jesus Christ, we are forgiven.*

EXHORTATION
Share the bread of forgiveness and the cup of salvation with others who are hungry and thirsty for God's love.

PRAYER OF THE DAY
Feeder of multitudes, enable us to find the hidden resources in ourselves and our neighbors, to share the spiritual food of your loving words, that the hungry in spirit do not go away searching aimlessly for that which will satisfy to all eternity, in the company of Jesus. Amen.

PRAYER OF THANKSGIVING
Unstinting Giver, eternal Gift, embracing Spirit, your love can conquer in all circumstances. You enable us to survive persecution with forgiveness. You give us patience to endure hardship. You grant us courage to face peril. Even death is overcome with resurrection. For such invaluable and imperishable gifts we are eternally grateful. Thanks be to you, O God, for your giving without stint. Thanks be to you, O Christ, for your death, resurrection and advocacy. Thanks be to you, family Spirit, for your unfailing love. Amen.

PRAYER OF DEDICATION

No gifts of ours, divine Giver, can be equated with yours. Multiply our offerings of hand and heart to satisfy the spiritual and physical needs of multitudes, to the glory of your name. Amen.

PSALM 143:1-10

Lord, hear my prayer, and in your faithfulness heed my supplications;

Answer me in your righteousness.

Enter not into judgment with your servant,

For in your sight shall no one living be justified.

For my enemy has sought my life; he has crushed me to the ground;

He has made me live in dark places like those who are long dead.

My spirit faints within me;

My heart within me is desolate.

I remember the time past; I muse upon all your deeds;

I consider the works of your hands.

I spread out my hands to you;

My soul gasps to you like a thirsty land.

O Lord, make haste to answer me; my spirit fails me;

Do not hide your face from me or I shall be like those who go down to the Pit.

Let me hear of your loving-kindness in the morning, for I put my trust in you;

Show me the road that I must walk, for I lift up my soul to you.

Deliver me from my enemies, O Lord,

For I flee to you for refuge.

Teach me to do what pleases you, for you are my God;

Let your good Spirit lead me on level ground.

TWELFTH SUNDAY AFTER PENTECOST

Exodus 14:19-31   Psalm 106:4-12
Romans 9:1-5   Matthew 14:22-33

CALL TO WORSHIP
Remember the many acts of God's faithful love. Believe the
promises of the eternal One and sing praises to God.

PRAYER OF CONFESSION
*God of all worlds, God of all weathers, God of all seasons, we
confess that we often look and listen for you in the wrong place or
with the wrong attitude. We are too easily moved by the many
voices of denial rather than by the lonely voices of truth, too
readily awed by the catastrophic and not by the quiet growth of
the living, too drawn to the fire of enthusiasms, too repelled by
the solitary duty you sometimes expect. Forgive the casual way
we throw in the towel when the opposition grows too strong.
Pardon the pride, the fear of failure and the fear of death that
prevent our full loyalty to the covenant you have made with us in
Jesus Christ. Amen.*

DECLARATION OF GOD'S FORGIVENESS
Hear the Good News! Deliverance is near to those who worship
God. Friends, believe the Good News. *In Jesus Christ, we are
forgiven.*

EXHORTATION
Take heart! Christ is with us in the Spirit. Do not be afraid. Go
when he calls you. Have faith that he will not let you down.

PRAYER OF THE DAY
*Son of God, in the midst of storm and strife, rough going and
contrary winds, come to assure us of your power and purpose,
that we may be saved to confess your name and be faithful in
following you wherever you lead us. Amen.*

PRAYER OF THANKSGIVING
*God of patriarchs and promises, Messiah to the temple and Christ
to the church, Holy Spirit, enlightening our consciences, we are
grateful for every experience of your presence and your help. We
bless you for the history of your people Israel, for the covenants
you made with them, for the psalms and promises and the
patience you have had with them and with us. We listen for you*

still, in the company of worshiping people and in the solitude of our lonely prayers, to discern your voice and identify your directions for us to take. We rejoice with apostles and prophets and all faithful people who praise your goodness and follow you in the way of peace; through Jesus Christ our Lord. Amen.

PRAYER OF DEDICATION
From the yields of the harvest and from the fruits of our labors, we bring you, supreme God, these offerings. Receive them as signs of our fidelity in response to the measure of prosperity you have permitted us; through Jesus Christ our Lord. Amen.

PSALM 106:4-12
Remember me, O Lord, with the favor you have for your people,
And visit me with your saving help;
That I may see the prosperity of your elect and be glad with the gladness of your people,
That I may glory with your inheritance.
We have sinned as our forebears did;
We have done wrong and dealt wickedly.
In Egypt they did not consider your marvelous works, nor remember the abundance of your love;
They defied the Most High at the Red Sea.
But he saved them for his Name's sake,
To make his power known.
He rebuked the Red Sea, and it dried up,
And he led them through the deep as through a desert.
He saved them from the hand of those who hated them
And redeemed them from the hand of the enemy.
The waters covered their oppressors;
Not one of them was left.
Then they believed his words
And sang him songs of praise.

THIRTEENTH SUNDAY AFTER PENTECOST

Exodus 16:2-15   Psalm 78:1-3, 10-20
Romans 11:13-16, 29-32   Matthew 15:21-28

CALL TO WORSHIP
Mark my teaching, O my people, listen to the words I am to speak. I will tell you a story with meaning, I will expound the riddle of things past, things that we have heard and known, and our parents have repeated to us.

PRAYER OF CONFESSION
God of all nations, your name is loved and hallowed in many languages. Yet nowhere in the world is your justice perfectly maintained and the right always done. We confess that we do not worship you in complete allegiance to your covenant with us nor in loving openness to all people of all nations, of all customs, of all conditions. We forget the mercy you have shown us in our time of disobedience and do not share your readiness to show mercy to those who are now disobedient. Forgive us for the sake of your all-loving Son, Jesus of Nazareth. Amen.

DECLARATION OF GOD'S FORGIVENESS
Hear the Good News! The gracious gifts of God and his calling are irrevocable. Friends, believe the Good News. *In Jesus Christ, we are forgiven.*

EXHORTATION
Show mercy as you have received mercy, for it is God's purpose to show mercy to all humanity.

PRAYER OF THE DAY
Son of David, Son of God, heal our souls, that we may be saved from our doubts and know the healing of faith that restores both us and those to whom you send us, of whatever nation or condition. Amen.

PRAYER OF THANKSGIVING
God of farmers and fishermen, we thank you for the harvest of the sea and the land, and for every wise plan of distribution that shares the plenty of the world with the greatest number of people, in this generation and those to come. God of all courts and legislatures, we are grateful for good laws and good decisions that overturn injustice and right wrongs, that protect the lives of the

*vulnerable and restrain the power of the ruthless. God of all
prophets and priests, we worship you whose face of truth and love
we have seen in Jesus Christ. We rejoice in the spread of the Good
News in the world by word and deed and celebrate your purpose
to show mercy to all humankind. All praise be given to you, God
of justice, God of salvation, God of mercy. Amen.*

PRAYER OF DEDICATION

*May our offerings and our prayers, universal God, be so generous
as to take in the needs of the whole world, and especially the
hungry, that our aid may seem like manna from heaven to those
who receive it, in the name of Jesus Christ. Amen.*

PSALM 78:1-3, 10-20

Hear my teaching, O my people;
Incline your ears to the words of my mouth.
I will open my mouth in a parable;
I will declare the mysteries of ancient times.
That which we have heard and known, and what our forefathers
     have told us,
We will not hide from their children.
They did not keep the covenant of God,
And refused to walk in his law;
They forgot what he had done,
And the wonders he had shown them.
He worked marvels in the sight of their forefathers,
In the land of Egypt, in the field of Zoan.
He split open the sea and let them pass through;
He made the waters stand up like walls.
He led them with a cloud by day,
And all the night through with a glow of fire.
He split the hard rocks in the wilderness
And gave them drink as from the great deep.
He brought streams out of the cliff,
And the waters gushed out like rivers.
But they went on sinning against him,
Rebelling in the desert against the Most High.
They tested God in their hearts, demanding food for their craving.
*They railed against God and said, "Can God set a table in the
     wilderness?*
True, he struck the rock, the waters gushed out, and the gullies
     overflowed;
But is he able to give bread or to provide meat for his people?"

FOURTEENTH SUNDAY AFTER PENTECOST

Exodus 17:1-7   Psalm 95
Romans 11:33-36   Matthew 16:13-20

CALL TO WORSHIP
The judgments of God are unsearchable, but search them out.
Continue to plumb the depths of God's wisdom and to trace the
ways of divine providence.

PRAYER OF CONFESSION
Source, Guide, and Goal of all that is, we acknowledge that
though we come from you, we have not always followed the
guidance you have given us in Jesus Christ. We have certainly not
reached the goal of perfection that lies ahead of us. Do not leave
unfinished the work you have begun in us. Though there is more
to know about you than we can ever learn, we are often distracted
from our search for the truth. Even when we have known Jesus to
be the way, we have been diverted by less strenuous climbs.
Though there are many awesome things in our world, we have not
seen beyond them to revere you. Be patient with us for the sake of
Jesus Christ, our older and wiser Brother. Amen.

DECLARATION OF GOD'S FORGIVENESS
Hear the Good News! God's true love endures forever and the
Lord will accomplish his purposes for us. Friends, believe the
Good News. *In Jesus Christ, we are forgiven.*

EXHORTATION
Let us confess in our own times that Jesus is the Messiah, the Son
of the living God. This is no longer a secret to be locked up, but a
door to be opened.

PRAYER OF THE DAY
Son of the living God, you have entrusted the keys of the kingdom
not merely to Peter, but to all who confess your name, for your
promises are as wide as the heavens. Prevent us from closing what
you want open and opening what you want closed according to
your wisdom and unfailing love. Amen.

PRAYER OF THANKSGIVING
God of all generations, God of prophets and apostles, God of
royalty and commoners, you are worshiped in tent and temple, in
chapel and cathedral. Your great glory is sung by the simple and

the wise, by poets and hymnists, by the untrained voice and the cultured singer. Your wisdom is sought by the illiterate and the widely-read, under the open heavens and in libraries and places of learning. We rejoice that though your wisdom is beyond our grasp, it has come within our reach in Jesus of Nazareth. Though your ways are untraceable, we may come to you by the way of Jesus, your Son and Son of Man. To you be glory forever. Amen.

PRAYER OF DEDICATION

Wise God, we can tell you only what you have taught us. Generous God, we can return to you only what you have already given us. Receive us and our gifts, for we have found our way to you through Jesus Christ. Amen.

PSALM 95

Come, let us sing to the Lord;
Let us shout for joy to the Rock of our salvation.
Let us come before his presence with thanksgiving
And raise a loud shout to him with psalms.
For the Lord is a great God,
And a great King above all gods.
In his hand are the caverns of the earth,
And the heights of the hills are his also.
The sea is his, for he made it,
And his hands have molded the dry land.
Come, let us bow down, and bend the knee,
And kneel before the Lord our Maker.
For he is our God,
And we are the people of his pasture and the sheep of his hand.
Oh, that today you would hearken to his voice!
Harden not your hearts, as your forebears did in the wilderness, at Meribah,
And on that day at Massah, when they tempted me.
They put me to the test, though they had seen my works.
Forty years long I detested that generation and said, "These people are wayward in their hearts; they do not know my ways."
So I swore in my wrath, "They shall not enter into my rest."

FIFTEENTH SUNDAY AFTER PENTECOST

Exodus 19:1-9   Psalm 114
Romans 12:1-13   Matthew 16:21-28

CALL TO WORSHIP

Let love for our community breed warmth of mutual affection.
With unflagging energy, in ardor of spirit, serve the Lord. Persist
in prayer.

PRAYER OF CONFESSION

*Thoughtful God, we confess that our thoughts are too content
with easy ways and the avoidance of suffering. Though you anoint
your people to the stresses of leadership, we prefer the safety of
obscurity. You sanctify us as prayerful priests to intercede for the
whole world. Too often we pray only for ourselves and not for the
nations around your earth. Forgive us for the sake of the cross-
bearing Christ. Amen.*

DECLARATION OF GOD'S FORGIVENESS

Hear the Good News. The Lord will redeem us and show us his
favor. Friends, believe the Good News. *In Jesus Christ, we are
forgiven.*

EXHORTATION

Adapt yourselves no longer to the pattern of this present world,
but let your minds be remade and your whole nature thus transformed. Then you will be able to discern the will of God.

PRAYER OF THE DAY

*God of the Gospel, Leader of disciples, Spirit of divinity and
humanity, plant the cross in our hearts, that our worldly
selfishness may die and our true self be raised from death to
heavenward life. Amen.*

PRAYER OF THANKSGIVING

*Faith-giving God, body-shaping Christ, nature-transforming Spirit,
we love the beauty of the body of Christ being transformed from
the uncoordinated movements of worldly behavior to the
choreography of obedience to your will. We listen with eagerness
to gifted voices that speak your gracious word. We work
enthusiastically with others who also seek to serve you and who
call out the best gifts we have been given. We worship you with
mind and body, as in Jesus Christ you have revealed your grace in*

his mind and body. We believe; we will obey; we are being changed thanks to you, loving God. Amen.

PRAYER OF DEDICATION

Uniting Christ, gather the varied personal gifts we bring into a functioning body, whose grace and accomplishments will be acceptable to you. Amen.

PSALM 114

Hallelujah! When Israel came out of Egypt,
The house of Jacob from a people of strange speech,
Judah became God's sanctuary
And Israel his dominion.
The sea beheld it and fled;
Jordan turned and went back.
The mountains skipped like rams,
And the little hills like young sheep.
What ailed you, O sea, that you fled?
O Jordan, that you turned back?
You mountains, that you skipped like rams?
You little hills like young sheep?
Tremble, O earth, at the presence of the Lord,
At the presence of the God of Jacob,
Who turned the hard rock into a pool of water
And flint-stone into a flowing spring.
You who fear the Lord, trust in the Lord; he is their help and their
    shield.

SIXTEENTH SUNDAY AFTER PENTECOST

Exodus 19:16-24   Psalm 115:1-11
Romans 13:1-10   Matthew 18:15-20

CALL TO WORSHIP
Be assured that the Lord is here. For Jesus said, "Where two or
three have met together in my name, I am there among them."

PRAYER OF CONFESSION
*Demanding God, loving God, holy God, we find it difficult to live
up to your expectations. You make loving our neighbor an
inescapable duty. We would rather be selective about our
relationships and limit our responsibilities to those with whom we
have a natural affinity. We do not like being corrected by others
and do not like to appear judgmental when we correct others. Is it
only prophets and rulers whom you call to be sentinels of the
moral security of the nation? Or will you hold us all accountable
if we do not speak out against evil? Forgive our silence if you have
prodded us to speak in your name, through Jesus Christ, Son of
Man, Son of God. Amen.*

DECLARATION OF GOD'S FORGIVENESS
Hear the Good News. The Lord will be good to his servants, as he
has promised. Friends, believe the Good News. *In Jesus Christ, we
are forgiven.*

EXHORTATION
Be under obligation to no one — the only obligation you have is
to love one another.

PRAYER OF THE DAY
*Heavenly Parent, Brother of sinners, Spirit in the church, help us
to agree in our prayers and in our common life that your purposes
may be accomplished, your will obeyed, and your children
reconciled to each other and gathered to Christ in the church.
Amen.*

PRAYER OF THANKSGIVING
*God of order, God of grace, God of the people, we are grateful for
the commandments you have given to order our common life. We
appreciate the teachings of Jesus as to how we are to interpret and
implement them. In seeking to be reconciled with those who have
sinned against us and with those against whom we have sinned,*

108

we are thankful for the aid of the Spirit. Grant that our happiness may always be in obedience to your commandments, in loving our neighbors as ourselves and loving you above all. We would be your obedient servants and loving children, a happy people gathering around the living Lord. Amen.

PRAYER OF DEDICATION
Lord of the church, receive our offerings as an expression of our love for you and for one another, that we may continue to gather here in your presence, to hear your word and to pray together. Amen.

PSALM 115:1-11
Not to us, O Lord, not to us, but to your Name give glory;
　　because of your love and because of your faithfulness.
Why should the heathen say, "Where then is their God?"
Our God is in heaven; whatever he wills to do he does.
Their idols are silver and gold, the work of human hands.
They have mouths, but they cannot speak;
Eyes have they, but they cannot see;
They have ears, but they cannot hear;
Noses, but they cannot smell;
They have hands, but they cannot feel;
Feet, but they cannot walk; they make no sound with their throat.
Those who make them are like them,
And so are all who put their trust in them.
O Israel, trust in the Lord; he is their help and their shield.
O house of Aaron, trust in the Lord; he is their help and their shield.

SEVENTEENTH SUNDAY AFTER PENTECOST

Exodus 20:1-20   Psalm 19:7-14
Romans 14:5-12   Matthew 18:21-35

CALL TO WORSHIP
Keep the Lord in mind as you honor the first day of the week as
the day of the resurrection.

PRAYER OF CONFESSION
*Father-in-Heaven, Brother-in-Heaven, mothering Spirit-Every-
where, we confess that we try your patience with our incon-
sistencies. We expect you to forgive our grossest sins, but
are unwilling to forgive the petty sins of our brothers and sisters,
our neighbors and friends. We recount for those closest to us the
number of times they have offended us, but forget the
numberless times you have forgiven us for a wide range of sins.
We want justice for our neighbor's misdemeanors, but mercy for
our own felonies. We do not have the same tolerance for others as
we have for ourselves. Forgive such unevenness, merciful God.
Amen.*

DECLARATION OF GOD'S FORGIVENESS
Hear the Good News! God pardons our guilt and surrounds us
with constant love, with tender affection. Friends, believe the
Good News. *In Jesus Christ, we are forgiven.*

EXHORTATION
Since God has not treated us as our sins deserve nor requited us
for our misdeeds, let us be forgiving, not only seven times, but
seventy times seven.

PRAYER OF THE DAY
*Holy Ruler, suffering Prince, saving Sovereign, persist in your
dealings with us until we have learned to forgive as you forgive
and to love our neighbors as we love ourselves, that your realm
may be extended from heaven to earth. Amen.*

PRAYER OF THANKSGIVING
*Universal God, from Greenwich to Greenwich, from pole to pole
to pole, you are our God and there is no other. There is no place
where we can escape your justice, but also no place where your
mercy does not reach. No journey into space can take us beyond
the bounds of your love. There are limits to our understanding of*

your ways in human history and endless questions, but your patience and love fill us with gratitude and praise. Glory to God in the highest. Glory to God on the earth. Glory to God in the church. Amen.

PRAYER OF DEDICATION

Let these offerings, divine Employer, be a sign of our service, that we do not live and do not work for ourselves alone, that whether we live or die we are yours. Amen.

PSALM 19:7-14

The law of the Lord is perfect and revives the soul;
The testimony of the Lord is sure and gives wisdom to the innocent.
The statutes of the Lord are just and rejoice the heart;
The commandment of the Lord is clear and gives light to the eyes.
The fear of the Lord is clean and endures for ever;
The judgments of the Lord are true and righteous altogether.
More to be desired are they than gold, more than much fine gold,
Sweeter far than honey, than honey in the comb.
By them also is your servant enlightened,
And in keeping them there is great reward.
Who can tell how often he offends?
Cleanse me from my secret faults.
Above all, keep your servant from presumptuous sins;
Let them not get dominion over me;
Then shall I be whole and sound, and innocent of a great offense.
Let the words of my mouth and the meditation of my heart be acceptable in your sight, O Lord, my strength and my redeemer.

EIGHTEENTH SUNDAY AFTER PENTECOST

Exodus 32:1-14   Psalm 106:7-8, 19-23
Philippians 1:21-27   Matthew 20:1-16

CALL TO WORSHIP

Add joy to your faith. Be one in spirit and one in mind, standing firm as you contend for the Gospel faith.

PRAYER OF CONFESSION

Owner of land and sea, Ruler of wind and wave, Spirit of Jesus Christ available to your people, we confess that we grumble about the work you give us to do, when it seems that we work longer and get no more reward than those who have not worked as long and hard. We have not always found joy in our work for its own sake nor rejoiced in what others have done, whether early or late. In the silence of this place, we acknowledge your right to do whatever you will with what is yours, but when our work and our life is tedious, we complain uncivilly. Forgive our disrespect for you and our disregard for the task you have given us to do. With the help of the Spirit, we may yet learn to find joy in your service. Amen.

DECLARATION OF GOD'S FORGIVENESS

Hear the Good News! Even when we do not remember God's acts of faithful love, our Savior delivers us for his name's sake. Friends, believe the Good News. *In Jesus Christ, we are forgiven.*

EXHORTATION

Add joy to your faith and let your conduct be worthy of the gospel of Jesus Christ.

PRAYER OF THE DAY

Heavenly Sovereign, save us from the jealousy that seeks to detract from the accomplishments of others, especially the young and those who have come late in life to your service, that all of us working together may find joy in serving you as one body, one in spirit, one in mind. Amen.

PRAYER OF THANKSGIVING

Who can count, gracious God, the times you have relented from destroying rebellious and stubborn people forgetful of your past mercies and turning to idolatry, the worship of lesser things? How often has a Moses thrown himself into the breach to save a nation! How grateful we are that your special child, Jesus, has done this for the whole world. We rejoice that whether we have come early or late to work for Christ in the church, you reward us beyond our deserving. Thanks be given to you, gracious God, mediating Christ, reconciling Spirit. Amen.

PRAYER OF DEDICATION

Patient God, may our offerings never be given as an excuse for indulgence after we have completed our Sunday service, but rather as a portion that signifies our discipline in worship and daily life, in the name of Jesus Christ. Amen.

PSALM 106:7-8, 19-23

In Egypt they did not consider your marvelous works, nor
    remember the abundance of your love:
They defied the Most High at the Red Sea.
But he saved them for his Name's sake,
To make his power known.
Israel made a bull-calf at Horeb and worshiped a molten image;
*And so they exchanged their Glory for the image of an ox that
    feeds on grass.*
They forgot God their Savior, who had done great things in
    Egypt,
*Wonderful deeds in the land of Ham, and fearful things at the
    Red Sea.*
So he would have destroyed them, had not Moses his chosen
    stood before him in the breach,
To turn away his wrath from consuming them.

NINETEENTH SUNDAY AFTER PENTECOST

Exodus 33:12-23
Philippians 2:1-13

Psalm 99
Matthew 21:28-32

CALL TO WORSHIP

Exalt our Sovereign God, and extol God's name, the One who is holy and mighty, who loves justice and forgives our misdeeds.

PRAYER OF CONFESSION

God who is, God who acts, God who moves others to act, you are righteous, principled in all you do, considerate in all you seek to accomplish with others. Our sins give evidence of the evil that is still a part of our nature. Our actions are often unprincipled, based on self-interest and showing little concern for the rights and feelings of others. We make promises we have no intention of keeping, simply evading an honest declaration of our priorities and commitments. We make excuses that are transparent to almost everyone but ourselves. We are ashamed to acknowledge our vanity and rivalry with others. Forgive our inordinate pride, our undependable word, our uncertain service, for the sake of your humble, dependable, and obedient servant and Son, Jesus the Christ. Amen.

DECLARATION OF GOD'S FORGIVENESS

Hear the Good News! God will hold innocent all who seek forgiveness of their misdeeds. Friends, believe the Good News. *In Jesus Christ, we are forgiven.*

EXHORTATION

Have the same love for one another. Look to each other's interests and not merely to your own. Have the same turn of mind and common care for unity.

PRAYER OF THE DAY

Deliver us, gracious Savior, from the delusion that only scandalous sinners need to repent and believe, so that by acknowledging our imperfections, we may change our minds and by believing more deeply, obey you more consistently. Amen.

PRAYER OF THANKSGIVING

Exalted Parent, humble and exalted Brother, shared Spirit, we rejoice in the story of Jesus of Nazareth. We revel in the mystery of his equality with you that he willingly abandoned for a time, to work as a slave to serve humanity's needs, to die as a criminal to

114

free us from our sins, to rise to glory and the exaltation of a name
that is more glorious than any other name. We praise you in the
world's greatest music and in the simplest words of children.
Receive our humble worship and sincere praise, today and always.
Amen.

PRAYER OF DEDICATION

No service of ours is too humble to offer to you, suffering Servant,
who, having served in earthly humility, has returned to the place
of heavenly honor. We offer you the best we can do. Amen.

PSALM 99

The Lord is King; let the people tremble;
He is enthroned upon the cherubim; let the earth shake.
The Lord is great in Zion;
He is high above all peoples.
Let them confess his Name, which is great and awesome;
He is the Holy One.
"O mighty King, lover of justice, you have established equity;
You have executed justice and righteousness in Jacob."
Proclaim the greatness of the Lord our God and fall down before
his footstool;
He is the Holy One.
Moses and Aaron among his priests, and Samuel among those
who call upon his Name,
They called upon the Lord, and he answered them.
He spoke to them out of the pillar of cloud;
They kept his testimonies and the decree that he gave them.
O Lord our God, you answered them indeed;
*You were a God who forgave them, yet punished them for their
evil deeds.*
Proclaim the greatness of the Lord our God and worship him
upon his holy hill;
For the Lord our God is the Holy One.

TWENTIETH SUNDAY AFTER PENTECOST

Numbers 27:12-23   Psalm 81:1-10
Philippians 3:12-21   Matthew 21:33-43

CALL TO WORSHIP

Invoke the God of the Gospel by name. Our Creator and
Redeemer will grant us new life in the Spirit.

PRAYER OF CONFESSION

*God of Israel, God of the church, God of all worlds, you gather
your people in order to cultivate in them the fruits of justice and
goodness. Too often we neglect our relationships in the
community so that it looks like an untended vineyard. We do not
sense the decline of faith and the loss of virtue that come without
the pruning disciplines of self-examination through the hearing of
your word of judgment and salvation. Forgive our laxity that
results in lack of spiritual fruitfulness. We should manifest the
graces of Jesus Christ. Amen.*

DECLARATION OF GOD'S FORGIVENESS

Hear the Good News! God calls us to the life above in Christ
Jesus. Friends, believe the Good News. *In Jesus Christ, we are
forgiven.*

EXHORTATION

Forget what is behind you and reach out to that which lies ahead,
the goal and the prize of heavenly glory in Christ Jesus.

PRAYER OF THE DAY

*Cornerstone of the church, remind us of who you are, that we may
never reject you and your claims for our reverence and obedience,
made known by prophets and apostles, who with us are built into
an abiding structure for your service among the nations. Amen.*

PRAYER OF THANKSGIVING

*God of the many and the few, God of the weak and the strong,
God of saints and sinners, we celebrate your patient care of your
people in all times and places. We rejoice in your continuing
patience with your people Israel. We are grateful for the broader
inclusiveness of the church of your Son, Jesus. How rich is the
spiritual heritage you have passed on to us through Judaism and
the Christian church! How challenging is the honorable task you
have given us to pass it on! Be near always to hear our thanks-*

givings with our prayers and petitions; through Jesus Christ our Lord. Amen.

PRAYER OF DEDICATION

Divine Sovereign, receive from us what is your due, not only these tokens from our hands, but the worship of our hearts, and the obedience of our daily lives and work, after the example of Jesus of Nazareth. Amen.

PSALM 81:1-10

Sing with joy to God our strength
And raise a loud shout to the God of Jacob.
Raise a song and sound the timbrel,
The merry harp, and the lyre.
Blow the ram's-horn at the new moon,
And at the full moon, the day of our feast.
For this is a statute for Israel,
A law of the God of Jacob.
He laid it as a solemn charge upon Joseph,
When he came out of the land of Egypt.
I heard an unfamiliar voice saying, "I eased his shoulder from the
    burden;
His hands were set free from bearing the load."
You called on me in trouble, and I saved you;
I answered you from the secret place of thunder and tested you at
    the waters of Meribah.
Hear, O my people, and I will admonish you:
O Israel, if you would but listen to me!
There shall be no strange god among you;
You shall not worship a foreign god.
I am the Lord your God, who brought you out of the land of
    Egypt and said,
"Open your mouth wide, and I will fill it."

TWENTY-FIRST SUNDAY AFTER PENTECOST

Deuteronomy 34:1-12   Psalm 135:1-14
Philippians 4:1-9   Matthew 22:1-14

CALL TO WORSHIP
My friends, all that is true, all that is noble, all that is just and
pure, all that is lovable and gracious, whatever is excellent
and admirable — fill all your thoughts with these things.

PRAYER OF CONFESSION
*Universal Sovereign, universal Prince, universal Spirit, you
provide us spiritual riches in great abundance. You are rightly
insulted by our indifference to your invitation to celebrate the
union of Christ and the church. We are undeserving of your
gracious invitation and often scandalized that you would accept
others we consider even less deserving. Forgive the rude treatment
that we have given your emissaries and our indifferent
preparedness when we do heed your invitation. Grant us time to
reconsider our priorities, to push aside more mundane things, and,
in giving first place to your rule, escape the judgment that would
otherwise await us. God, have mercy on us; Christ, have mercy on
us; Holy Spirit, be merciful to us. Amen.*

DECLARATION OF GOD'S FORGIVENESS
Hear the Good News! The peace of God, which is beyond our
understanding, will keep our hearts and our thoughts, in
Christ Jesus. Friends, believe the Good News. *In Jesus Christ, we
are forgiven.*

EXHORTATION
Put into practice all that you have received from the Christian
tradition, what you have heard and what you have seen done by
Christians who have set an example for you.

PRAYER OF THE DAY
*Attending Spirit, prepare us for fellowship with the Son of heaven
and our royal Parent, so that, clothed in the beauty of holiness, we
may enjoy the heavenly feast that celebrates the victory of Christ
over sin and death. Amen.*

PRAYER OF THANKSGIVING
God of Moses and of Miriam his sister, you are worshiped not

only in psalms, but in tambourine dance, for you free the enslaved and bring them out to freedom. Christ Jesus, founder of the church, we rejoice that the names of all who struggle in the cause of the Gospel are in the roll of the living. Timeless Spirit, you bring together into one people those who gather at Sinai and Philippi. We rejoice that you can make community of those who have been in conflict, both in the process of time and the climax of history. Your name, O God, endures forever. Amen.

PRAYER OF DEDICATION

As we stand in your house, O God, we present these tokens of our servanthood. We would serve you both in worship and in the cause of human justice with Jesus Christ, who practices what he preaches. Amen.

PSALM 135:1-14

Hallelujah! Praise the Name of the Lord;
Give praise, you servants of the Lord;
You who stand in the house of the Lord,
In the courts of the house of our God.
Praise the Lord, for the Lord is good;
Sing praises to his Name, for it is lovely.
For the Lord has chosen Jacob for himself
And Israel for his own possession.
For I know that the Lord is great,
And that our Lord is above all gods.
The Lord does whatever pleases him, in heaven and on earth,
In the seas and all the deeps.
He brings up rain clouds from the ends of the earth;
He sends out lightning with the rain, and brings the winds out of his store house.
It was he who struck down the firstborn of Egypt,
The firstborn both of man and beast.
He sent signs and wonders into the midst of you, O Egypt,
Against Pharaoh and all his servants.
He overthrew many nations
And put mighty kings to death:
Sihon, king of the Amorites, and Og, the king of Bashan,
And all the kingdoms of Canaan.
He gave their land to be an inheritance,
An inheritance for Israel his people.
O Lord, your Name is everlasting;
Your renown, O Lord, endures from age to age.
For the Lord gives his people justice
And shows compassion to his servants.

TWENTY-SECOND SUNDAY AFTER PENTECOST

Ruth 1:1-19a   Psalm 146
1 Thessalonians 1:1-10   Matthew 22:15-22

CALL TO WORSHIP
Put no faith in princes, but in the Creator who also watches over
the stranger, and gives heart to the orphan and widow.

PRAYER OF CONFESSION
*Creator of heaven and earth, Maker of all humanity, Judge of all
persons; hear our confession. Though we worship you now, we
frequently show more respect for powerful political figures than
for you. We are more concerned about the bills we owe to the tax
collector and to business people than what we owe to you and
your church, both in money and in personal service. Though you
have made us in your likeness, we behave as if we are self-made
and with no obligation to please you, our Maker, and no duty to
serve you, our Teacher, and no accountability to you, our Judge.
Forgive our false claims to what is yours and our ungrateful use
and abuse of your creation, for the sake of Jesus Christ, our Savior.
Amen.*

DECLARATION OF GOD'S FORGIVENESS
Hear the Good News! Brothers and sisters beloved by God, who
has chosen you and sent the Good News to you, receive the
divine gifts of grace and peace. Friends, believe the Good News.
In Jesus Christ, we are forgiven.

EXHORTATION
Show your faith in action, your love in labor, and your hope in
courage. Live in the power of the Holy Spirit, with strong
conviction.

PRAYER OF THE DAY
*Sovereign above all sovereigns, clarify our vision of your majesty,
that all worldly powers may appear in proper proportion to your
authority, and our allegiances duly ordered, so that we may give
you and our neighbor what is due, in the spirit of Jesus Christ.
Amen.*

PRAYER OF THANKSGIVING
*Living and true God, we praise your name and give thanks for all
who have spread faith in your name. We rejoice in the victory of*

Jesus over death and in our deliverance from the terrors of judgment to come. We celebrate the persuasive power of the Spirit to strengthen our convictions and enable our service. We are grateful for all the ties of love and friendship that cross tribal lines and language barriers, recovering the unity of the human family. With the whole brotherhood and sisterhood of Jesus Christ, we praise you, paternal, fraternal, maternal God. Amen.

PRAYER OF DEDICATION

Empowering Spirit, strengthen our convictions, that we may always give God what is due to God and to governments what is due to governments and to your church what is due to your church; through Jesus Christ our Lord. Amen.

PSALM 146

Hallelujah!
Praise the Lord, O my soul!
I will praise the Lord as long as I live;
I will sing praises to my God while I have my being.
Put not your trust in rulers, nor in any child of earth, for there is
    no help in them.
*When they breathe their last, they return to earth, and in that day
    their thoughts perish.*
Happy are they who have the God of Jacob for their help!
Whose hope is in the Lord their God;
Who made heaven and earth, the seas, and all that is in them;
Who keeps his promise for ever;
Who gives justice to those who are oppressed, and food to those
    who hunger.
The Lord sets the prisoners free;
The Lord opens the eyes of the blind;
The Lord lifts up those who are bowed down;
The Lord loves the righteous; the Lord cares for the stranger;
*He sustains the orphan and widow, but frustrates the way of the
    wicked.*
The Lord shall reign for ever,
Your God, O Zion, throughout all generations. Hallelujah!

TWENTY-THIRD SUNDAY AFTER PENTECOST

Ruth 2:1-13   Psalm 128
1 Thessalonians 2:1-8   Matthew 22:34-46

CALL TO WORSHIP
Revere our Sovereign God. There are many blessings in store for those who honor God and do the will of our Sovereign.

PRAYER OF CONFESSION
God of high places, God of low places, God of all places, we confess that we are not full of compassion as you are. We are prone to forget what it is like to be aliens, to be powerless, to be vulnerable, to be without an advocate, to be without credit. Forgive our complicity in heartless systems that make credit cheap and easy for those who need it least and prohibitive for those who need it most. Forgive indifference toward, or ill treatment of, widows and orphans when we forget that they could be our own widows and orphans. We need to repent of all our less-than-loving behavior and attitudes for the sake of your all-loving Son, Jesus of Nazareth. Amen.

DECLARATION OF GOD'S FORGIVENESS
Hear the Good News! God has approved us as fit to be entrusted with the Gospel. Friends, believe the Good News. *In Jesus Christ, we are forgiven.*

EXHORTATION
Love our Sovereign God with all your heart and soul and mind and your neighbor as yourself.

PRAYER OF THE DAY
Loving God, captivate our emotions in the worship of you, integrate our personhood in communion with you and make us wise in the knowledge of you, that we may love ourselves truly and our neighbor in the same way, like our loving Brother, Jesus Christ. Amen.

PRAYER OF THANKSGIVING
God of strength and gentleness, we rejoice in the gentleness we see in those who care fondly for children. We are grateful for the deliberate beneficence of those who have more than they need and provide for those who are needy. We are thankful for those who use their power not to exploit others, but to defend and

protect those who are vulnerable to exploitation. We are glad to honor all who declare the Good News of Jesus Christ without base motives of greed or hunger for power. Help us always to seek only your favor and to pass every test of our motives in serving others, as did Jesus Christ, our example. Amen.

PRAYER OF DEDICATION
Receive our gifts and ourselves, Sovereign God, so that we may be faithful envoys of the Good News and the witness of our church be fruitful, with your help. Amen.

PSALM 128
Happy are they all who fear the Lord,
And who follow in his ways!
You shall eat the fruit of your labor;
Happiness and prosperity shall be yours.
Your wife shall be like a fruitful vine within your house,
Your children like olive shoots round about your table.
The man who fears the Lord shall thus indeed be blessed.
The Lord bless you from Zion, and may you see the prosperity of
    Jerusalem all the days of your life.
May you live to see your children's children;
May peace be upon Israel.

TWENTY-FOURTH SUNDAY AFTER PENTECOST

Ruth 4:7-17   Psalm 127
1 Thessalonians 2:9-13, 17-20   Matthew 23:1-12

CALL TO WORSHIP
Receive God's message, not as the word of men, but as what it
truly is, the very word of God at work in you who hold the faith.

PRAYER OF CONFESSION
*Heavenly Parent, strong as any father, gentle as any mother, we
are dependent on you for both life and sustenance. Forgive our
moments of pride when we act as if we did not need you. Rabbi
above all other rabbis, Teacher above all teachers, forgive us if at
times we act like know-it-alls, unteachable and dogmatic about
what we do and do not believe. Supreme Leader, anointed One,
forgive any move we make to displace you, whether in exalting
ourselves in places of authority or in giving to others the honor
due only to you. Be patient with us, as a parent dealing with
immature children, for the sake of your mature Child, Jesus Christ.
Amen.*

DECLARATION OF GOD'S FORGIVENESS
Hear the Good News! Those who humble themselves will be
exalted. Friends, believe the Good News from God! *In Jesus
Christ, we are forgiven.*

EXHORTATION
Achieve true greatness. Be a willing servant of those around you
who are your brothers and sisters.

PRAYER OF THE DAY
*By your words and by your lifestyle, teach us, Rabbi-Messiah, to
speak your word graciously and to serve others humbly, that we
may not exalt ourselves only to be brought low by your judgment.
Amen.*

PRAYER OF THANKSGIVING
*Gracious God, we thank you for your call to enter into your
kingdom and glory. We are grateful that your living word is at
work in us to prepare us for worthy service in your realm. We
express our thanksgiving for the advice and encouragement of our
fathers and mothers and our brothers and sisters in the faith, and
all who have imparted to us your Good News. We will show our*

gratitude by committing ourselves to others in the same kind of caring ministry, sharing your loving word, through Jesus Christ our Lord. Amen.

PRAYER OF DEDICATION

O God, help us to give and live, worthy of the call into your realm of glory through Jesus Christ our Lord. Amen.

PSALM 127

Unless the Lord builds the house, their labor is in vain who build it.

Unless the Lord watches over the city, in vain the watchman keeps his vigil.

It is in vain that you rise so early and go to bed so late;

Vain, too, to eat the bread of toil, for he gives to his beloved sleep.

Children are a heritage from the Lord,

And the fruit of the womb is a gift.

Like arrows in the hand of a warrior are the children of one's youth.

Happy is the man who has his quiver full of them!

HE SHALL NOT BE PUT TO SHAME WHEN HE CONTENDS WITH HIS ENEMIES IN THE GATE.

TWENTY-FIFTH SUNDAY AFTER PENTECOST

Amos 5:18-24   Psalm 50:7-15
1 Thessalonians 4:13-18   Matthew 25:1-13

CALL TO WORSHIP
Offer to God the sacrifice of thanksgiving and pay your vows to
the Most High.

PRAYER OF CONFESSION
*God of the unchanging and the unexpected, we are hard-put to
know what the day of the Lord is, let alone when it may come.
Much of life seems cyclical, going around and around and not
moving in any perceptible direction. Justice seems less like a
flowing river and more like a fountain that occasionally rises to
great heights, only to subside again. Forgive us if we are more
curious than concerned, more puzzled than prepared for your
judgments whenever they come. Prepare us for the day of Christ's
coming, in our death or in human history. Amen.*

DECLARATION OF GOD'S FORGIVENESS
Hear the Good News! We believe that Jesus died and rose again;
and so it will be for those who died as Christians; God will bring
them to life with Jesus. Friends, believe the Good News. *In Jesus
Christ, we are forgiven.*

EXHORTATION
Keep awake in the spirit, for you never know when the day or
hour of the Lord will come.

PRAYER OF THE DAY
*Ruler of heaven, grant us prudence in our preparation for your
coming, that we may know what gifts of the Spirit are needed, if
we are to be ready to greet you with confidence and rejoicing.
Amen.*

PRAYER OF THANKSGIVING
*God of the unchanging and the unexpected, we are grateful for
constants in nature on which we can usually depend. We are
thankful also for the unexpected that wakes us to the reality of
your expectations. We appreciate the warnings that come in times
of danger or sickness or accident, that remind us of our mortality
and our need to be prepared for the kingdom still to come. May all
the beauties and bounties of the natural world create in us a*

FILED

longing for the beauty and bounty of the eternal realm to which you bring all who look for it, through Jesus Christ. Amen.

PRAYER OF DEDICATION

Self-sufficient God, there is nothing we can bring to you that you need, for all is already yours. You have come to our rescue again and again, so we merely honor you by these tokens of appreciation, through Jesus Christ our Lord. Amen.

PSALM 50:7-15

Hear, O my people, and I will speak:
"O Israel, I will bear witness against you; for I am God, your God.
I do not accuse you because of your sacrifices;
Your offerings are always before me.
I will take no bull-calf from your stalls,
No he-goats out of your pens;
For all the beasts of the forest are mine,
The herds in their thousands upon the hills.
I know every bird in the sky,
And the creatures of the fields are in my sight.
If I were hungry, I would not tell you,
For the whole world is mine and all that is in it.
Do you think I eat the flesh of bulls,
Or drink the blood of goats?
Offer to God a sacrifice of thanksgiving
And make good your vows to the Most High.
Call upon me in the day of trouble;
I will deliver you, and you shall honor me."

TWENTY-SIXTH SUNDAY AFTER PENTECOST

Zephaniah 1:7, 12-18   Psalm 76
1 Thessalonians 5:1-11   Matthew 25:14-30

CALL TO WORSHIP

Make vows to our Sovereign God and pay them duly. Let all
people bring their tribute to the heavenly Sovereign.

PRAYER OF CONFESSION

*God of fire and fury, God of mercy and salvation, who can stand
in your presence when you are angry? You may rightly give
sentence out of heaven, declaring judgment on kings and queens,
on nobility as well as commoners. And yet you send prophets and
apostles with words of warning, that we may repent of our sins
and, turning from them, find mercy and salvation. Forgive our
waste of time and of opportunities to improve our readiness for
the coming of our Savior, Jesus Christ. Amen.*

DECLARATION OF GOD'S FORGIVENESS

Hear the Good News! God has not ordained us to the terrors of
judgment, but to the full attainment of salvation through our
Lord Jesus Christ. Friends, believe the Good News. *In Jesus Christ,
we are forgiven.*

EXHORTATION

Hearten one another and fortify one another in the faith that we
may live in company with Jesus Christ.

PRAYER OF THE DAY

*Divine Executive, remind us of our obligations to you so that we
will not waste opportunities to use, to the advantage of heaven,
the assets you have given us and be found empty-handed in the
end. Amen.*

PRAYER OF THANKSGIVING

*God of creativity, we acknowledge with wonder the gifts and
talents you have given to human beings. What magnificent works
of music have been composed and performed by many in
centuries of productivity! What beautiful sanctuaries have been
built to the glory of your name! What proliferations of hospitals
and other institutions of healing have been raised by your
inspiration! The unnumbered varieties of great works in writing
and learning, on tapestry and canvas, are returns on the gifts you*

have given. We thank you for the opportunity of serving you with whatever talents we have, and ask that you receive them by the grace of our Lord Jesus Christ. Amen.

PRAYER OF DEDICATION

Sovereign God, you are properly honored with the tributes of the great and the small, by the famous and the unknown. Receive what we offer as tokens of our faithful use of whatever talents you have given us, to the honor of your name. Amen.

PSALM 76

In Judah is God known;
His Name is great in Israel.
At Salem is his tabernacle,
And his dwelling is in Zion.
There he broke the flashing arrows,
The shield, the sword, and the weapons of battle.
How glorious you are!
More splendid than the everlasting mountains!
The strong of heart have been despoiled; they sink into sleep;
None of the warriors can lift a hand.
At your rebuke, O God of Jacob, both horse and rider lie stunned.
*What terror you inspire! who can stand before you when you are
    angry?*
From heaven you pronounced judgment;
The earth was afraid and was still;
When God rose up to judgment
And to save all the oppressed of the earth.
Truly, wrathful Edom will give you thanks,
And the remnant of Hamath will keep your feasts.
Make a vow to the Lord your God and keep it;
Let all around him bring gifts to him who is worthy to be feared.
He breaks the spirit of princes,
And strikes terror in the kings of the earth.

TWENTY-SEVENTH SUNDAY AFTER PENTECOST
CHRIST THE KING

Ezekiel 34:11-16, 20-24   Psalm 12
1 Corinthians 15:20-28   Matthew 25:31-46

CALL TO WORSHIP

Welcome to this house of the Lord, and be at home here and wherever God's flock is gathered.

PRAYER OF CONFESSION

Shepherd-God, strong and gentle, you have as Creator authority to judge between the nations as sheep and goats and to judge the flock of Israel as well. We confess that though we count ourselves in your flock, we are sometimes unaware of the rude way we push aside those less strong than ourselves. Sometimes our criticisms are so brutal as to drive away those who need the protection of the fold. Forgive such haughtiness and hardheartedness that can ravage your flock from within and scatter them from your fold, for the sake of Jesus, the Good Shepherd, who comes in search of us. Amen.

DECLARATION OF GOD'S FORGIVENESS

Hear the Good News! The risen Christ is destined to reign until God has put all enemies under his feet, and the last enemy to be abolished is death. Friends, believe the Good News! *In Jesus Christ, we are forgiven.*

EXHORTATION

Feed the hungry, give drink to the thirsty, take in the stranger, clothe the naked, heal the sick and visit the prisoner, for in doing this you serve the Sovereign, Christ.

PRAYER OF THE DAY

Child of glory, Son of Man, grant us the blessing of the eternal Parent as we follow your example of loving service to all in need, and receive us into the community that has been made ready for us since the world was made. Amen.

PRAYER OF THANKSGIVING

God of power, Champion of the weak, Spirit of freedom, we rejoice in your continuing involvement with the struggles and conflicts of our world. Through the death and resurrection of Jesus, you promise the final abolition of death. The Spirit of

130

freedom inspires the overthrow of every tyranny over the mind
and the spirit of humanity. We celebrate the victory still to come,
when all such tyrants shall be defeated and the whole world is
delivered up to the One-above-all. Thanksgiving and honor and
glory we give to the God of justice and mercy, of loving and
caring, of striving and winning. Amen.

PRAYER OF DEDICATION
Universal God, we are dedicated to do for you what is within our
personal capacity to do, and also, through our offerings, what we
can only do together, not only in this place, but across the nation
and around the world, to the glory of your hallowed name. Amen.

PSALM 12
Help me, Lord, for there is no godly one left;
The faithful have vanished from among us.
Everyone speaks falsely with his neighbor;
With a smooth tongue they speak from a double heart.
Oh, that the Lord would cut off all smooth tongues,
And close the lips that utter proud boasts!
Those who say, "With our tongue will we prevail;
Our lips are our own; who is lord over us?"
"Because the needy are oppressed,
And the poor cry out in misery,
I will rise up" says the Lord,
"And give them the help they long for."
The words of the Lord are pure words,
Like silver refined from ore and purified seven times in the fire.
O Lord, watch over us and save us from this generation for ever.
*The wicked prowl on every side, and that which is worthless is
   highly prized by everyone.*

ALL SAINTS' DAY

Revelation 7:9-17   Psalm 34:1-10
1 John 3:1-3   Matthew 5:1-12

CALL TO WORSHIP
Fear our God, all you holy people, for all those who fear him lack
nothing. Those who seek God lack no good thing.

PRAYER OF CONFESSION
*God of all nations and tribes and peoples and languages, we admit
to saying things we do not mean, sometimes out of fear,
sometimes out of the intention to deceive. We have denied the
faith and acted as though we are godless, in order to live
undetected among the irreligious. We have been implicated in
unrighteous causes, rather than oppose them and risk persecution.
We have advocated war and not peace, revenge rather than
mercy, aggressiveness and not gentleness. Our only blessedness is
the need for you and for your goodness, which you will satisfy by
the spirit of Jesus Christ. Amen.*

DECLARATION OF GOD'S FORGIVENESS
Hear the Good News! How blest are those who show mercy;
mercy shall be shown to them. Friends, believe the Good
News! *In Jesus Christ, we are forgiven.*

EXHORTATION
Be purified in the hope of seeing Christ as he is, and being like
him, pure and loving.

PRAYER OF THE DAY
*Great Discipler, draw us closer around you, that we may learn
from you what true blessedness is, so that we will leave behind all
lesser things, in the strong desire to be included in the community
of all your people. Amen.*

PRAYER OF THANKSGIVING
*How great is the love God has shown to us in calling us children!
How numerous are the tribes and nations God has sealed to
belong to the eternal empire! How exciting are the prospects of
seeing Christ as he is and being like him! For hopes of such
blessedness, we give thanks to you, O God. For clearer visions of
who you are and what we will be like, we give thanks and praise
your name, royal Jesus. For mercy and consolation, for cleansing*

and salvation, we give thanks and exult in your saving power, divine Spirit. Amen.

PRAYER OF DEDICATION

Who but an understanding parent could receive such humble gifts as we bring to you, O God? We come to you in the worthiness of your perfect Child, Jesus Christ, and in his name. Amen.

PSALM 34:1-10

I will bless the Lord at all times;
His praise shall ever be in my mouth.
I will glory in the Lord;
Let the humble hear and rejoice.
Proclaim with me the greatness of the Lord;
Let us exalt his Name together.
I sought the Lord, and he answered me
And delivered me out of all my terror.
Look upon him and be radiant,
And let not your faces be ashamed.
I called in my affliction and the Lord heard me and saved me
   from all my troubles.
*The angel of the Lord encompasses those who fear him, and he
   will deliver them.*
Taste and see that the Lord is good;
Happy are they who trust in him!
Fear the Lord, you that are his saints,
For those who fear him lack nothing.
The young lions lack and suffer hunger,
But those who seek the Lord lack nothing that is good.

THANKSGIVING DAY

Deuteronomy 8:7-18   Psalm 65
2 Corinthians 9:6-15   Luke 17:11-19

CALL TO WORSHIP
Let us enjoy the blessing of God's house, and be happy that we
have been invited here.

PRAYER OF CONFESSION
*God of creation, God of order, God of love, we can forget to be
thankful, not only when taking for granted your many provisions
for us in nature, but even in the critical times of health restored
and difficulties overcome. Forgive the pride that assumes that we
are more deserving than others, and the conceit that what we do
well is without any aid from others or from you. Save us from the
sin of ingratitude, through your modest and thankful Child, Jesus
of Nazareth. Amen.*

DECLARATION OF GOD'S FORGIVENESS
Hear the Good News! Though our sins are too heavy for us, God
can blot them out, as we lay our guilt before him. Friends,
believe the Good News. *In Jesus Christ, we are forgiven.*

EXHORTATION
Share what you have with others, meeting their need with your
surplus. It is a question of equality, not hardship, and expected
by our Creator.

PRAYER OF THE DAY
*God creating, God healing, God sharing, remind us when we have
taken for granted any of your good gifts, natural, spiritual,
intellectual, so that we may manifest a thankful spirit, both in our
prayers and in our relations with others, through the prompting of
the Spirit of Jesus Christ. Amen.*

PRAYER OF THANKSGIVING
*Grand Designer, mighty Maker, personable Spirit, all nature
praises you. The skies celebrate your majesty in a choreography of
clouds and sun, light and shadow, sunshine and rain, moonlight
and stars, and with the soaring of birds. The seas are orchestrated
in your praise by the movements of the tides, the thunder of the
surf, the splash of fish. The earth sings with the woodwinds of the
forest, the song of birds, the voices of creatures without words, as
well as singers of many languages. They are echoed in valleys and*

beamed and broadcast by human technology. We are awed by the intricacy of your plans. We are humbled by the powers of energy and mass. We respond, however imperfectly, to your love in nature and in Jesus Christ, your Child and our Brother. We give thanks to you, O God, Thinker, Doer, Lover. Amen.

PRAYER OF DEDICATION

Help us always to give with a generous spirit, Lord Jesus, remembering that though you were rich, you became poor, that we through your poverty might become rich. Amen.

PSALM 65

You are to be praised, O God, in Zion;
To you shall vows be performed in Jerusalem.
To you that hear prayer shall all flesh come, because of their transgressions.
Our sins are stronger than we are, but you will blot them out.
Happy are they whom you choose and draw to your courts to dwell there!
They will be satisfied by the beauty of your house, by the holiness of your temple.
Awesome things will you show us in your righteousness, O God of our salvation,
O Hope of all the ends of the earth and of the seas that are far away.
You make fast the mountains by your power;
They are girded about with might.
You still the roaring of the seas,
The roaring of their waves, and the clamor of the peoples.
Those who dwell at the ends of the earth will tremble at your marvelous signs;
You make the dawn and the dusk to sing for joy.
You visit the earth and water it abundantly;
You make it very plenteous; the river of God is full of water.
You prepare the grain,
For so you provide for the earth.
You drench the furrows and smooth out the ridges;
With heavy rain you soften the ground and bless its increase.
You crown the year with your goodness;
And your paths overflow with plenty.
May the fields of the wilderness be rich for grazing,
And the hills be clothed with joy.
May the meadows cover themselves with flocks,
And the valleys cloak themselves with grain; let them shout for joy and sing.

INDEX OF THE SCRIPTURE PASSAGES

Genesis
2:4b-9, 15-17, 25, 3:1-7   44
12:1-8   46
12:1-9   79
22:1-18   81
25:19-34   83
28:10-17   85
32:22-32   87

Exodus
1:6-14, 1:22-2:10   89
2:11-22   91
3:1-12   93
3:13-20   95
12:1-14   97
14:19-31   99
16:2-15   101
17:1-7   103
17:3-7   48
19:1-9   105
19:16-24   107
20:1-20   109
24:12-18   40
32:1-14   111
33:12-23   113

Leviticus
19:1-2, 9-18   38

Numbers
27:12-23   115

Deuteronomy
4:32-40   77
8:7-18   133
30:15-20   34
34:1-12   117

Ruth
1:1-19a   119
2:1-13   121
4:7-17   123

1 Samuel
16:1-13   50

Psalms
2:6-11   40
11   17
13   81

16:5-11   61
17:1-7, 15   87
19:7-14   109
23   50, 65
24   9
27:1-6   28
29   24
31:1-8   67
31:9-16   54
33   77
33:12-22   79
33:18-22   46
34:1-10   131
37:1-11   30
40:1-11   26
46   83
47   71
50:7-15   125
51:1-12   42
62   129
62:5-12   36
65   133
66:8-20   69
68:1-10   73
69:6-15   91
72:1-8   5
72:1-14   21
76   127
78:1-3, 10-20   101
80:1-10   115
91:1-10   85
95   48, 103
96   11
97   13
98   15
99   113
103:1-13   93
104:24-33   75
105:1-11   95
106:7, 8, 19-23   111
106:4-12   99
112:4-9   32
114   105
115:1-11   107
116:1-9   52
116:12-19   63
118:14-24   59
118:19-29   56
119:1-8   34
119:33-40   38

136

122	3	3:13-17	24
124	89	4:1-11	44
127	123	4:12-23	28
128	121	5:1-12	30,31
130	44	5:13-16	32
135:1-14	117	5:17-26	34
143:1-10	97	5:27-37	36
146	119	5:38-48	38
146:5-10	7	6:1-6, 16-18	42
147:12-20	19	7:21-29	79
		9:9-13	81

Isaiah

		9:35-10:8	83
2:1-5	3	10:24-33	85
7:10-16	9	10:34-42	87
9:1-4	28	11:2-11	7
9:2-7	11	11:25-30	89
11:1-10	5	13:1-9, 18-23	91
35:1-6, 10	7	13:24-30, 36-43	93
42:1-9	24	13:44-52	95
44:1-8	75	14:13-21	97
49:1-7	26	14:22-33	99
49:8-13	36	15:21-28	101
50:4-9a	54, 56	16:13-20	103
52:7-10	15	16:21-28	105
58:3-10	32	17:1-9	40,46
60:1-6	21	18:15-20	107
62:6-7, 10-12	13	18:21-35	109
63:7-9	17	20:1-16	111
		21:1-11	56

Jeremiah

		21:12-17	58
31:1-6	59	21:18-27	58
31:7-14	19	21:28-32	113
		21:33-43	115

Ezekiel

		22:1-14	117
34:11-16, 20-24	129	22:15-22	119
37:1-14	52	22:34-56	121
		23:1-12	123

Joel

		23:29-24:8	58
2:12-18	42	24:36-44	3
		25:1-13	125

Amos

		25:14-30	127
5:18-24	125	25:31-46	129
		26:1-16	58

Micah

		26:14-17, 66	54
6:1-8	30	26:17-30	58
		26:30-56	58

Zephaniah

		26:57-75	58
1:7, 12-18	127	27:1-10	58
		27:11-31	58

Matthew

		27:32-54	58
1:18-25	9	27:55-56	58
2:1-12	21	28:1-10	59
2:13-15	17	28:11-20	61
2:19-23	17	28:16-20	77
3:1-12	5		

Luke
2:1-20 — 11
2:8-20 — 13
17:11-19 — 133
24:13-35 — 63
24:46-53 — 71

John
1:1-14 — 15
1:1-18 — 19
1:29-34 — 26
3:1-7 — 46
4:5-26 — 48
7:37-39 — 75
9:1-41 — 50
10:1-10 — 65
11:1-16, 17-45 — 52
12:12-16 — 56
14:1-14 — 67
14:15-21 — 69
17:1-11 — 73
20:1-9 — 59
20:19-31 — 61

Acts
1:1-11 — 71
1:6-14 — 73
2:1-21 — 75
2:14a, 22-32 — 61
2:14a, 36-41 — 63
2:42-47 — 65
7:55-60 — 67
10:34-43 — 24, 59
17:22-31 — 69

Romans
1:1-7 — 9
3:21-28 — 79
4:1-5, 13-16a — 46
4:13-18 — 81
5:6-11 — 83
5:12-19 — 44, 85
6:3-11 — 87
7:14-25a — 89
8:6-11 — 52
8:9-17 — 91
8:18-25 — 93
8:31-39 — 97
9:1-5 — 99
11:13-16, 29-32 — 101
11:33-36 — 103
12:1-13 — 105
13:1-10 — 107
13:11-14 — 3

14:5-12 — 109
15:4-13 — 5

1 Corinthians
1:1-9 — 26
1:10-17 — 28
1:18-31 — 30
2:1-11 — 32
3:1-9 — 34
3:10-11, 16-23 — 36
4:1-5 — 38
12:3b-13 — 75
15:20-28 — 129

2 Corinthians
5:20-6:2 — 42
9:6-15 — 133
13:5-14 — 77

Ephesians
1:3-6, 15-18 — 19
1:15-23 — 71
3:1-6 — 21
5:8-14 — 50

Philippians
1:21-27 — 111
2:1-13 — 113
2:5-11 — 54, 56
3:12-21 — 115
4:1-9 — 117

Colossians
3:1-4 — 59

1 Thessalonians
1:1-10 — 119
2:1-8 — 121
2:9-13, 17-20 — 123
4:13-18 — 125
5:1-11 — 127

Titus
2:11-14 — 11
3:4-7 — 13

Hebrews
1:1-12 — 15
2:10-18 — 17

James
5:7-10 — 7

1 Peter

1:3-9	61
1:17-21	63
2:2-10	67
2:19-25	65
3:13-22	69
4:12-14	73
5:6-11	73

2 Peter

1:16-21	40

1 John

3:1-3	131

Revelation

7:9-17	131